D1577711

Atelier 26 Books

Regeneration Series

The heavens stood over the heads
of our ancestors as near as to us.
Any living word in their books
abolishes the difference of time.
—Henry David Thoreau
   Dec. 14, 1841

this is
A26/RS 1

Caricature of Thoreau by Daniel Ricketson, 1856

Henry David Thoreau

HENRY DAVID THOREAU was born in Concord Massachusetts on July 12, 1817 and christened David Henry Thoreau. He attended school in Concord, went to Harvard University in 1833, and graduated in 1837. That year he read Ralph Waldo Emerson's *Nature*, probably heard Emerson deliver "The American Scholar" as an address to Harvard's Phi Beta Kappa Society, became a personal friend of the older writer (who had moved to Concord a few years prior), and at Emerson's recommendation began to keep a journal. In search of an occupation, Thoreau taught school in Concord, but resigned after two weeks in protest against being forced to administer corporal punishment on six students in a single afternoon. He changed the order of his first and middle names and in 1838 delivered his first lecture, "Society," at the Concord Lyceum. That same year, he returned to teaching, this time on his own terms, establishing a school and incorporating into his pedagogy the revolutionary concepts of recess and field trips. In 1840 his first published work appeared in the inaugural issue of *The Dial*, under the editorship of Margaret Fuller. With the closure of his school in 1841, Thoreau moved into the Emerson family home, earning room and board as the family's groundskeeper and handyman. In early 1842, Thoreau's beloved brother John, age 27, died of lockjaw after cutting his finger with a razor. John's death profoundly affected Henry and would influence some of his major life decisions. Thoreau moved to Staten Island in 1843 to live with the family of William Emerson, the writer's brother, and serve as tutor for his three sons, but he found life in New York disagreeable. For a short time while there, he sold magazine subscriptions door-to-door. Within seven months, he had returned to Concord, and would never again live beyond its environs. During 1844 he worked in earnest at the Thoreau family's pencil factory behind their Concord home, helping to improve the materials and means of production for the graphite pencil cores. On July 4, 1845 Thoreau moved into a 10-foot by 15-foot cabin he'd built himself on the small east cove of Concord's Walden Pond. The cabin, situated on a parcel of land owned by Emerson, was Thoreau's residence for two years, two months, and two days, during which time he drafted his first book *A Week on the Concord and Merrimack Rivers* in memory of his brother, and wrote large portions of what would become his masterpiece, *Walden.* On a July day in 1846 while walking to town to have a shoe mended, Thoreau was arrested and held for one night in the Concord jail for refusal to pay his poll tax. He explained that he could not in good conscience underwrite slavery and the Mexican-American War with his own money. He was released the following day when an unknown person paid the tax on his behalf. The jailing episode resulted in Thoreau's seminal essay "Civil Disobedience," first delivered as a lecture in 1848. Mohandas Ghandi, John F. Kennedy, Martin Luther King, Jr., Leo Tolstoy, and many others have credited "Civil Disobedience" as a major influence. Upon leaving

Walden, Thoreau returned to the Emerson family home, helping Mrs. Emerson manage the household while her husband lectured in Europe. A year later he relocated to the upstairs bedroom of the Thoreau family home on Concord's Main Street, where he would live the rest of his life, earning wages from surveying, general handywork, and his occasional lectures and magazine publications. Thoreau made extended excursions to Cape Cod, the Maine wilderness, and Quebec, and reflected on these travels in his writings. He was acquainted with many literary figures in his day, including Nathaniel Hawthorne, the Alcott family, the James family, Walt Whitman, and Horace Greeley. He was instrumental in the Underground Railroad in Concord and lectured in defense of the militant abolitionist John Brown in the weeks preceding Brown's execution by the U.S. government. He spent the greater part of his time walking in the woods and fields surrounding Concord, and recording his philosophy and natural observations in the journal he'd started in 1837. His almost daily journal entries span the course of 25 years and amount to roughly two million words. *Walden* was finally published in August of 1854. Though for the most part critically well-received, by 1859 the book had only sold around 2,000 copies. Thoreau died of tuberculosis in early 1862 at age 44, having just completed his final essay "Walking," in which appear the words "In wildness is the preservation of the world."

Edited by M. Allen Cunningham

FUNNY-ASS
THOREAU

✳   ✳   ✳

ATELIER26 : Regeneration Series, Vol. 1
Portland, Oregon

Cover design by Nathan Shields
Book design by M.A.C.

Funny-Ass Thoreau
Regeneration Series, Vol. 1

isbn-13: 978-0-9893023-8-8
isbn-10: 0-9893023-8-5

Library of Congress Control Number:
2016953606

The valued support of Sidney Wade
helped make this book possible.

Atelier26 Books are printed in the U.S.A. on
acid-free paper

Atelier26

"A magnificent enthusiasm, which feels
as of it never could do enough to reach
the fullness of its ideal; an unselfishness
of sacrifice, which would rather cast
fruitless labour before the altar than
stand idle in the market."
—John Ruskin

Atelier26Books.com

By spells seriousness will be forced to cut capers,
and drink a deep refreshing draught of silliness.
… I exult in stark inanity.

—Henry David Thoreau,
Journal, January 24, 1841

CONTENTS

Introduction:
The Stand-Up Philosopher

When I was fourteen my mother, exasperated by the onset of my teenage angst, handed me a Penguin paperback of Thoreau's *Walden* and said, "Read this. The guy who wrote it was a rebel like you." For some reason, I did as she suggested, and in *Walden's* transcendental rants I found all my angsty teenage convictions gloriously and authoritatively ratified. Institutions were bad: they wanted to straitjacket my thoughts and crush my creativity; my elders were either corrupt or absent-mindedly hypocritical, either tyrannical or brainwashed, tragic or just pitiful; the dictates of fashion and good form were stifling and almost always ridiculous; money was a golden calf, prosperity overrated, and "making a good living" was a fool's errand; as for our so-called government, it was just one big immoral business.

It was all there in Thoreau. On institutions: "Wherever a man goes, men will pursue and paw him with their dirty institutions, and, if they can, constrain him to belong to their desperate odd-fellow society."

And concerning one's elders: "One generation abandons the enterprises of another like stranded vessels."

And about the absurdity of fashions: "We know but few men, a great many coats and breeches. … The head monkey at Paris puts on a traveller's cap, and all the monkeys in America do the same."

And regarding materialism: "A man is rich in proportion to the number of things which he can afford to let alone." "Give me the poverty that enjoys true wealth."

And about the corruption of government: "The only true America is that country where...the state does not endeavor to compel you to sustain...slavery and war and other superfluous expenses."

And all this in a book that was one hundred and forty years old! Could my mother have known, as she plunked down $8.95 for that crisp paperback with its innocuous cover (Lady Liberty in an eighteenth-century allegorical painting), that she was financing the most significant turn in her son's life? The pliable goop of my pre-frontal cortex could not have met with any text more salutary to that hour in my development and its obsessions.

But it wasn't just *Walden*'s relentless exposure of every innately North American hypocrisy that caused me — like so many young people before and after me — to adopt it as a gospel; it was also the things the book extolled: the ideal of liberty, the beauty of being out of step, the value of standing aside and taking one's time, our all-encompassing quotidian natural wonders. *Walden* was as much a spiritualized embrace of a few choice things as a sneering rejection of others. Even here, though, my adoption of the book was more blindly evangelical than truly comprehending. I needed so badly to attach myself to an idealized Thoreau and ventriloquize through that fearlessly eloquent, time-tested voice — and so keenly did I embody Erikson's fifth developmental stage (identity vs. identity confusion) — that I was neurologically incapable of any lucid appreciation of just what Thoreau *the writer* was up to.

Young people, despite their flippant veneers, tend to be terribly earnest — and to flatten into earnestness material that is much more richly nuanced. Subtleties and subtexts aren't their thing. And it's mostly young people, we should now admit, who have inadvertently done Thoreau a disservice.

Since around the centennial of his death in the early 1960s, when the advent of the Beats and Civil Rights and Environmentalism engendered a new attachment to Walden's bygone prophet, we've made such good use of old Henry as mouthpiece for one worthy cause or another that we've lost all perspective on his marvelous authorial range. In particular, we've totally failed to get his jokes.

For me, Thoreau's writing was a drug. It knocked my neurons around. It worked me over completely, induced a sort of insanity, and actually changed the course of my life forever. And still, until quite recently, I did not get the jokes. Had you taken the pains to point out to me, at fourteen, the extent of the levity that permeates *Walden* and much of Thoreau's writing, I might have punched you in the nose. You see, my upbringing was not only religious, but of the proselytizing kind, and that fervor was still in my bones. None of us at church, incidentally, got the jokes in Jesus either. Beam in the eye? Camel through a needle?

Sheeps and goats? You could cue us with a high-hat and snare — *ba-dum-chah!* — but beyond the ensuing song of crickets all you'd get back was grim reverence. Our common assumption was that if one was talking of serious things (in Jesus' case, salvation of the soul; in Thoreau's, a secular version of the same), one could only do so, well, seriously.

But though at fourteen I wished to believe otherwise, Thoreau never intended for *Walden* to serve as a self-help manual for virtuous living. His intention was to arrive at certain inalienable truths, but his means of getting there was often oblique rather than direct, and always more artful than strictly autobiographical. He was no social architect, had no such pretensions, and thus was not in the business of issuing blueprints. Throughout his body of writing he relied on exaggeration, sarcasm, paradox, and aphoristic hyperbole over straightforward statement. He frequently opted for the literary and allusive over the literal. And he larded his lines with puns and submerged secondary meanings that frequently aimed for laughs. Depicting himself ironically well-employed as nature's surveyor and inspector in *Walden*'s first chapter, he boasts: "I have watered the red huckleberry, the sand cherry and the nettle tree, the red pine and the black ash, the white grape and the yellow violet, which might have withered else in dry seasons." Like much of *Walden*'s wit, the Falstaffian irreverence here, wherein Thoreau confesses to being a serial outdoor pisser, went — to deploy a pun of my own — whizzing right over the teenage reader's head.

Strangely enough, during Henry's lifetime his problem was precisely the opposite: his audience had learned to anticipate laughs whenever he appeared in print or rose to speak. Thoreau was reputed to be a humorist (it was by that term that Nathaniel Hawthorne described him in a letter to a friend), and on the lyceum circuit he tended to crack up the crowds. Following lectures in Salem and Gloucester in 1848, the reviews were unanimous. His Salem talk, as reported in the local *Observer*, was "done in an admirable manner, in a strain of exquisite humor, with a strong undercurrent of delicate satire against the follies of the times. Then there were the interspersed observations, speculations, and suggestions upon dress, fashions, food, dwellings, furniture, &c., &c., sufficiently queer to keep the audience in almost constant mirth…The performance has created 'quite a sensation' amongst lyceum goers." Gloucester's *Telegraph* also lauded his humor, noting his facility for: "'bringing down the house' by his quaint remarks." In both places, he had lectured from what would become *Walden*'s overture, "Economy," which today is popularly (and unjustly) considered a dry and over-long barrier to entry for new readers of the book.

Following his public successes, Thoreau was importuned for more of the same. "Curators of lyceums write to me," he noted in his journal. "DEAR SIR, — I hear that you have a lecture of some humor. Will you do us the favor to read it before the Bungtown Institute?"

He was a comic savant for hire, or so they hoped. At the lectern or not, he tended to give the impression that he was kidding around. After *Walden*'s 1854 publication, Thoreau bemusedly recorded in the journal that a friend of Emerson had been "much interested in my *Walden*, but relished it merely as a capital satire and joke, and even thought that the survey and map of the pond were not real, but a caricature of the Coast surveys."

In the journal in 1855, Henry homed in on his own penchant for planting tongue in cheek:

> My faults are: —
> Paradoxes, — saying just the opposite, —
> a style which might be imitated.
> Ingenious.
> Playing with words, — getting the laugh,
> — not always simple, strong, and broad.
> Using current phrases and maxims, when
> I should speak for myself.
> Not always earnest.

How can we square these facts with Thoreau's more current reputation? For alongside the idolators and pedestal-makers, Henry has his haters, and one of their favorite complaints is that he was all scowling prophecy, zero funnybone. These dour literalists would show us in *Walden* and Thoreau's other works a pouting town pariah, a preachy puritan whose proto-tiny-house experiment in living was no more than a white man's delusional holiday, a mean little humorless bastard of a scourge on par with Dickens' Scrooge, and/or a wannabe woodsman disingenuously fortified, in his rustic cabin, by pies from Mom's kitchen.

This species of attack can be traced backed to 1865, just three years after Thoreau's death, in a scathing article by James Russell Lowell, one of Thoreau's erstwhile magazine editors. Writing in the *North American Review*, Lowell grumbled:

> He seems to me to have been a man with so high a conceit of himself that he accepted without questioning, and insisted on our accepting, his defects and weaknesses of character as virtues and powers peculiar to himself. … Thoreau seems to have prized a lofty way of thinking (often we should be inclined to call it a remote one) not so much because it was good in itself as because he wished few to share it with him. … He seeks, at all risks, for perversity of thought. … Mr. Thoreau seems to me to insist in public on going back to flint and steel, when there is a match-box in his pocket which he knows very well how to use at a pinch. … Mr. Thoreau had not a healthy mind, or he would not have been so fond of prescribing. His whole life was a search for the doctor. … Thoreau had no humor, and this implies that he was a

sorry logician. ... There is something delight-
fully absurd in six volumes addressed to a
world of such 'vulgar fellows' as Thoreau
affirmed his fellow men to be. I once had a
glimpse of a genuine solitary who spent his
winters one hundred and fifty miles beyond
all human communication, and there dwelt
with his rifle as his only confidant. Compared
with this, the shanty on Walden Pond has
something the air, it must be confessed, of the
Hermitage of La Chevrette.

But roughly halfway through his screed, Lowell
discredits himself with a more sweeping complaint, and
we catch the dull shimmer of the axe he really wishes to
grind:

I look upon a great deal of the modern senti-
mentalism about Nature as a mark of disease.
It is one more symptom of the general liver-
complaint. To a man of wholesome constitu-
tion the wilderness is well enough for a mood
or a vacation, but not for a habit of life. ... It
is a very shallow view that affirms trees and
rocks to be healthy, and cannot see that men
in communities are just as true to the laws of
their organization and destiny. ... To hear
the to-do that is often made over the simple
fact that a man sees the image of himself in
the outward world, one is reminded of a

savage when he for the first time catches a
glimpse of himself in a looking-glass.

Here we might have excused the counsel from
trying this particular literary case. But Lowell's words
saw print, and lo, point by point (e.g. "[Thoreau]
squatted on another man's land; he borrow[ed] an
axe") his deprecation has spawned innumerable little
Lowells ever since — a recent so-called "takedown" of
Thoreau in *The New Yorker* is only the youngest of the
clutch, and bears all the predictable birthmarks.

Still, while such philippics crop up with boring
semi-annual regularity, Thoreau's standing in our literature is unshaken. And as we continue to read him, he
will continue to be many things to many people —
wonderfully so. Speaking to change-makers and ecolo-
gists, rainbow-tog Buddhists and curriculum commit-
tees, his work is vast in its importance and appeal. And
yet, having planted our peace flags, hiking boots, and
sundry other emblems and totems in the fecund soil of
his pond-side ode to nonconformity, let's take care not
to reduce the richness of Thoreau's literary genius and
flatten out our sense of his roundness as a writer.

Let us remember, especially, how funny he could be
— how alive to the special force of wisecracking wit.
Here he is, for instance, in the chapter of *Walden* called
"Reading":

I confess I do not make any very broad
distinction between the illiterateness of my

townsmen who cannot read at all, and the
illiterateness of him who has learned to read
only what is for children and feeble intellects.
We should be as good as the worthies of
antiquity, but partly by first knowing how
good they were. We are a race of tit-men, and
soar but little higher in our intellectual flights
than the columns of the daily paper.

And in the chapter called "Solitude":

Society is commonly too cheap. We meet at
very short intervals, not having had time to
acquire any new value for each other. We
meet at meals three times a day, and give each
other a new taste of that old musty cheese
that we are.

And in "Visitors":

I had more visitors while I lived in the woods
than at any other period of my life; I mean
that I had some.

And in "Economy":

Probably I should not consciously and
deliberately forsake my particular calling to
do the good which society demands of me, to
save the universe from annihilation; and I

believe that a like but infinitely greater steadfastness elsewhere is all that now preserves it.

And in his journal:

The merchants and banks are suspending and failing all the country over, but not the sand banks, solid and warm. ... You may run on them as much as you please, — even as the crickets do, and find their account in it. ... In these banks, too, and such as these, are my funds deposited, funds of health and enjoyment. (October 14, 1857)

There is some advantage in being the humblest, cheapest, least dignified man in the village, so that the very stable boys shall damn you. Methinks I enjoy that advantage to an unusual extent. (July 6, 1851)

He is often at his most sparkling when describing animals, as in this 1857 journal entry:

I hear the alarum of a small red squirrel. I see him running by fits and starts along a chestnut bough toward me. His head looks disproportionately large for his body, like a bulldog's, perhaps because he has his chaps full of nuts. ... He finds noise and activity for both of us. It is evident that all this ado does not proceed from fear. There is at the bottom, no doubt, an excess of inquisitiveness and caution, but the greater part is make-believe, and a love of the marvelous. He can hardly keep it up till I am gone, however, but takes out his nut and tastes it in the midst of his agitation. *"See there, see there,"* says he, "who's that? O dear, what shall I do?" and makes believe run off, but does n't get along an inch, — lets it all pass off by flashes through his tail, while he clings to the bark as if he were holding in a race-horse. He gets down the trunk at last upon a projecting knot, head downward, within a rod of you, and chirrups and chatters louder than ever. Tries to work himself into a fright. The hind part of his body is urging the forward part along, snapping the tail over it like a whip-lash, but the fore part, for the most part, clings fast to the bark with desperate energy. (October 5, 1857)

What misanthrope writes like that?

Let's bear in mind that Transcendentalism, beyond being a nineteenth-century pseudo-religion concerned with abolitionism and utopian farming communities (and long, long before it meant self-congratulatory hallucinogenic trips), was a *literary-aesthetic* movement. Its writers were practitioners of craft above all else.

They knew what they were about on every page. Thoreau "shaped *Walden* specifically with his contemporary readers in mind," writes David S. Reynolds in *Beneath the American Renaissance: The Subversive Imagination in the Age of Emerson and Melville.* "His adaptation of popular humor was an intrinsic element of his self-appointed mission to absorb the language of common Americans and make it the vehicle of uplifting notions about individualism and deliberate living. More frequently than any American writer of the period — more frequently, even, than Emerson — Thoreau underscored the necessity for persons of genius to incorporate into their style the popular idioms of their own time and culture. ... The humor of *Walden* is indeed popular humor, but it is popular humor carefully transformed by a philosopher who wishes to salvage both his culture and his culture's favorite images."

Does it seem superficial to plead for appreciation of Thoreau's stylistic range, and to do so now, in our apocalyptic days of social and climatological unrest, when it is his *messages* — "In wildness is the preservation of the world," etc. — that remain so urgent and resonant? The thing is, despite our contemporary enshrinement of "Content" as the keyword of progress, popularity, and profit, what makes a work of literature lasting is its *form* as much as what it contains. The order, shape, and semi-secret palimpsest of meanings matters. The design matters. That is to say, the art and discipline of literature matters.

In our understanding of old Henry, prophetic exponent of simplicity, what seems called for is an injection of salubrious *complexity*. This was no wannabe woodsman nor failed hermit nor mama's boy. This was a writer. Generation after generation since Lowell, Thoreau's haters have insisted on "exposing" him as fake, "unlikeable," or humorless because they fail to grasp the distinction between literary license and the literal, or to appreciate his complex identity as an artist — that is, as a creator of literary conceits.

Is it because he sneered at so many of our still precious constructs that they love to sneer back at the construct of his masterful book? For artistic construct — deep, painstakingly developed, and nearly ten years in the writing — is what *Walden* has been all along. Ralph Waldo Emerson spoke to this aspect of Thoreau's vision in the eulogy for his friend: "There was an excellent wisdom in him, proper to a rare class of men, which showed him the material world as a means and symbol. ... The tendency to magnify the moment, to read all the laws of nature in the one object or one combination under your eye. ... The pond was a small ocean; the Atlantic, a large Walden Pond. He referred every minute fact to cosmical laws."

From *Walden*'s opening pages Thoreau himself pitches the book's whole premise at the level of parable:

> I long ago lost a hound, a bay horse, and a
> turtle-dove, and am still on their trail. Many
> are the travellers I have spoken concerning
> them, describing their tracks and what calls

they answered to. I have met one or two who had heard the hound, and the tramp of the horse, and even seen the dove disappear behind a cloud, and they seemed anxious to recover them as if they had lost them themselves.

And in the following, which comes roughly at *Walden*'s midpoint, he lays bare the entire conceit. Just look at how he draws the world's immensity into the luminous exurban environs of the book as into a visionary crystal ball:

There is commonly sufficient space about us. Our horizon is never quite at our elbows. The thick wood is not just at our door, nor the pond, but somewhat is always clearing, familiar and worn by us, appropriated and fenced in some way, and reclaimed from Nature. For what reason have I this vast range and circuit, some square miles of unfrequented forest, for my privacy, abandoned to me by men? My nearest neighbor is a mile distant, and no house is visible from any place but the hill-tops within half a mile of my own. I have my horizon bounded by woods all to myself; a distant view of the railroad where it touches the pond on the one hand, and of the fence which skirts the woodland road on the other. But for the most part it is as solitary where I live as on the prairies. It is as much Asia or Africa as New England. I have, as it were, my own sun and moon and stars, and a little world all to myself. At night there was never a traveller passed my house, or knocked at my door, more than if I were the first or last man.

And at *Walden's* close, quite deliberately, Thoreau disowns the role of exemplar, thus discouraging the reader from taking his account too much at face value, as some kind of sociological reform paper:

I left the woods for as good a reason as I went there. Perhaps it seemed to me that I had several more lives to live, and could not spare any more time for that one. It is remarkable how easily and insensibly we fall into a particular route, and make a beaten track for ourselves. I had not lived there a week before my feet wore a path from my door to the pond-side; and though it is five or six years since I trod it, it is still quite distinct. It is true, I fear that others may have fallen into it, and so helped to keep it open.

"*Walden* aims at conversion," noted John Updike. But this is true only insofar as we mean conversion of the mystic and personal order: introspective realization, not outward revolution. Inward moral clarity at the level of the individual situated within the natural world, not a holy-minded movement en masse. Thoreau never saw a crowd he could trust or would care to join. He'd said it in the first chapter, too:

> I would not have anyone adopt *my* mode of living on any account; for, besides that before he has fairly learned it I may have found out another for myself, I desire that there be as many different persons in the world as possible; but I would have each one be careful to find out and pursue his *own* way, and not his father's or his mother's or his neighbor's instead.

There it is, kids. And lest any of you aged fourteen or younger are now rowing out upon the rippling and prismatic infinities of Thoreau's work, I wish you the best on what may become a lifelong exploration. Like Walden Pond itself, rumored in his time to have no bottom, old Henry won't be plumbed. But I beg you, please, please give the guy some credit by laughing as you sink your line.

This volume marks the first of its kind: a compendium of some of Thoreau's funniest passages. Here he is taming a woodchuck or adopting a screech owl, playing checkers with a loon or consoling himself on losing a tooth, in hot pursuit of an escaped pig or narrowly evading arrest on suspicion of bank robbery. Here too are sketches of the Concord villagers, of whom he is obviously fond, much as he may delight in unhasping their clock-doors to poke at their cogs and sprockets. As I've assembled this book, extracting Thoreau's most iridescent moments and shuffling them up side by side, I've sensed in the project something recuperative and just, especially now on the eve of the 2017 bicentennial of his birth. True, it's taken us a little too long to get here, but I invite you to read this book the Thoreauvian way: in full defiance of preconceptions about the man. Throughout these pages Thoreau provokes our laughter while dazzling us anew with the singular esprit of his prose. We find him as alive and vivacious as he ever was — and what a kick to read.

—M. ALLEN CUNNINGHAM
Portland, Oregon, summer 2016

FUNNY-ASS
THOREAU

*   *   *

What Befell at Mrs. Brooks's

On the morning of the 17th Mrs. Brooks's Irish girl Joan fell down the cellar stairs, and was found by her mistress lying at the bottom, apparently lifeless. Mrs. Brooks ran to the street-door for aid to get her up, and asked a Miss Farmer, who was passing, to call the blacksmith near by. The latter lady turned instantly, and, making haste across the road on this errand, fell flat in a puddle of melted snow, and came back to Mrs. Brooks's, bruised and dripping and asking for opodeldoc.[1] Mrs. Brooks again ran to the door and called to George Bigelow to complete the unfinished errand. He ran nimbly about it and fell flat in another puddle near the former, but, his joints being limber, got along without opodeldoc and raised the blacksmith. He also notified James Burke, who was passing, and he, rushing in to render aid, fell off one side of the cellar stairs in the dark. They no sooner got the girl upstairs than she came to and went raving, then had a fit.

Haste makes waste. It never rains but it pours. I have this from those who have heard Mrs. Brooks's story, seen the girl, the stairs, and the puddles.

Journal: March 19, 1856

---

[1] A liniment containing camphor and alcohol

Take Them All

Dr. Ware Jr. said today in his speech at the meeting house — "There are these three — Sympathy — Faith — Patience" — then proceeding in ministerial style, "and the greatest of these is," but for a moment he was at a loss, and became a listener along with his audience, and concluded with "Which is it? I don't know. Pray take them all brethren, and God help you."

Journal: November 4, 1840

Advantage

There is some advantage in being the humblest, cheapest, least dignified man in the village, so that the very stable boys shall damn you. Methinks I enjoy that advantage to an unusual extent.

Journal: July 6, 1850

They

It is desirable that a man be clad so simply that he can lay his hands on himself in the dark, and that he live in all respects so completely and preparedly, that, if an enemy take the town, he can, like the old philosopher, walk out the gate empty-handed without anxiety. ... When I ask for a garment of a particular form, my tailoress tells me gravely, "They do not make them so now," not emphasizing the "They" at all, as if she quoted an authority as impersonal as the Fates, and I find it difficult to get made what I want, simply because she cannot believe that I mean what I say, that I am so rash. When I hear this oracular sentence, I am for a moment absorbed in thought, emphasizing to myself each word separately that I may come at the meaning of it, that I may find out by what degree of consanguinity *They* are releated to *me*, and what authority they may have in an affair which affects me so nearly; and, finally, I am inclined to answer her with equal mystery, and without any more emphasis of the "they,"—"It is true, they did not make them so recently, but they do now."

Walden, "Economy"

Waldo's Cows

I was amused by R.W.E.'s[2] telling me that he drove his own calf out of the yard, as it was coming in with the cow, not knowing it to be his own, a drove going by at the time.

Journal: December 8, 1854

Waldo's Wheelbarrow

I doubt if Emerson could trundle a wheelbarrow through the streets, because it would be out of character. One needs to have a comprehensive character.

Journal: January 30, 1852

Duck Character

Two ducks, of the summer or wood species, which were merrily dabbling in their favorite basin, struck up a retreat on my approach, and seemed disposed to take

---

[2] Ralph Waldo Emerson

French leave, paddling off with swan-like majesty. They are first-rate swimmers, beating me at a round pace, and — what was to me a new trait in the duck character — dove every minute or two and swam several feet underwater, in order to escape our attention. Just before immersion they seemed to give each other a significant nod, and then, as if by a common understanding, 't was heels up and head down in the shaking of a duck's wing. When they reappeared, it was amusing to observe with what self-satisfied, darn-it-how-he-nicks-'em air they paddled off to repeat the experiment.

Journal: October 29, 1837

Turtle-Walk

A turtle walking is as if a man were to try to walk by sticking his legs and arms merely out the windows.

Journal: May 27, 1853

Hat Vapors

I am inclined to think that my hat, whose lining is gathered in midway so as to make a shelf, is about as good a botany-box as I could have and far more convenient, and there is something in the darkness and the vapors that arise from the head — at least if you take a bath — which preserves flowers through a long walk. Flowers will frequently come fresh out of this botany-box at the end of the day, though they have had no sprinkling.

Journal: June 23, 1852

Seed Concussions

The touch-me-not seed-vessels go off like pistols, — shoot their seeds off like bullets. They explode in my hat.

Journal: September 27, 1852

Henry the Bee

The scenery, when it is truly seen, reacts on the life of the seer. How to live. How to get the most life. How to extract its honey from the flower of the world. That is my everyday business. I am as busy as a bee about it. I ramble over all fields on that errand, and am never so happy as when I feel myself heavy with honey and wax. I am like a bee searching the livelong days for the sweets of nature. Do I not impregnate and intermix the flowers, produce rare and finer varieties by transferring my eyes from one to another? I do as naturally and as joyfully, with my own humming music, seek honey all the day. With what honeyed thought any experience yields me I take a bee line to my cell. It is with flowers I would deal.

Journal: September 7, 1851

Old People

What old people say you cannot do you try and find that you can. Old deeds for old people, and new deeds for new. Old people did not know enough once, perchance, to fetch fresh fuel to keep the fire a-going; new people put a little dry wood under a pot, and are whirled round the globe with the speed of birds, in a way to kill old people, as the phrase is. Age is no better, hardly so well, qualified for an instructor as youth, for it has not profited so much as it has lost. One may almost doubt if the wisest man has learned anything of absolute value by living. Practically, the old have no very important advice to give the young, their own experience has been so partial, and their lives have been such miserable failures, for private reasons, as they must believe; and it may be that they have some faith left which belies that experience, and they are only less young than they were. I have lived some thirty years on this planet, and I have yet to hear the first syllable of valuable or even earnest advice from my seniors. They have told me nothing, and probably cannot tell me anything, to the purpose. Here is life, an experiment to a great extent untried by me; but it does not avail me that they have tried it. If I have any experience which I think valuable, I am sure to reflect that this my Mentors said nothing about.

One farmer says to me, "You cannot live on vegetable food solely, for it furnishes nothing to make bones with;" and so he religiously devotes a part of his day to supplying his system with the raw materials of bones; walking all the while he talks behind his oxen, which, with vegetable-made bones, jerk him and his lumbering plough along in spite of every obstacle. Some things are really necessaries of life in some circles, the most helpless and diseased, which in others are luxuries merely, and in others still are entirely unknown.

Walden, "Economy"

Behaved

The greater part of what my neighbors call good I believe in my soul to be bad, and if I repent of anything, it is very likely to be my good behavior. What demon possessed me that I behaved so well?

Walden, "Economy"

Better the Dentist than the Priest

If I have got false teeth, I trust that I have not got a false conscience. It is safer to employ the dentist than the priest to repair the deficiencies of nature.

By taking the ether the other day I was convinced how far asunder a man could be separated from his senses. You are told that it will make you unconscious, but no one can imagine what it is to be unconscious — how far removed the state of consciousness and all that we call "this world" — until he has experienced it. The value of the experiment is that it does give you experience of an interval between one life and another, — a greater space than you ever traveled. You are a sane mind without organs, — groping for organs, — which if it did not soon recover its old senses would get new ones. You expand like a seed in the ground. You exist in your roots, like a tree in the winter. If you have an inclination to travel, take the ether; you go beyond the furthest star.

It is not necessary for them to take ether, who in their sane and waking hours are ever translated by a thought; not for them to see with their hindheads, who sometimes see with their foreheads; nor listen to the

spiritual knockings, who attend to the intimations of
reason and conscience.

Journal: May 12, 1851

When I Took the Ether

When I took the ether my consciousness amounted to
this: I put my finger on myself in order to keep the
place, otherwise I should never have returned to this
world.

Journal: January 26, 1856

Birdlike

Saw a shrike pecking to pieces a small bird, apparently a
snow bird. At length he took him up in his bill, almost
half as big as himself, and flew slowly off with his prey
dangling from his beak. I find that I had not associated
such actions with my idea of birds. It was not birdlike.

Journal: December 24, 1850

On Cape Cod, Part 1:
Not Any's Representatives

When the committee from Plymouth had purchased the
territory of Eastham of the Indians, "it was demanded,
who laid claims to Billingsgate?" which was understood
to be all that part of the Cape north of what they had
purchased. "The answer was, there was not any who
owned it. 'Then,' said the committee, 'that land is ours.'
The Indians answered that it was." This was a remarkable assertion and admission. The Pilgrims appear to
have regarded themselves as Not Any's representatives.

Perhaps this was the first instance of that quiet way of "speaking for" a place not yet occupied, or at any least not improved as much as it may be, which their descendants have practiced, and are still practicing so extensively. Not Any seems to have been the sole proprietor of all America before the Yankees.

Cape Cod

Useful, Beautiful Ignorance

I have heard that there is a Society for the Diffusion of Useful Knowledge. It is said that knowledge is power and the like. Methinks there is equal need of a Society for the Diffusion of Useful Ignorance, for what is most of our boasted so-called knowledge but a conceit that we know something, which robs us of the advantages of our actual ignorance.

For a man's ignorance sometimes is not only useful but beautiful, while his knowledge is oftentimes worse than useless, besides being ugly. In reference to important things, whose knowledge amounts to more than a consciousness of his ignorance? Yet what more refreshing and inspiring knowledge than this?

Journal: February 9, 1851

Min's Adventures, Part 1

Our kitten Min, two-thirds grown, was playing with Sophia's[3] broom this morning, as she was sweeping the parlor, when she suddenly went into a fit, dashed round

---

[3] Henry's younger sister Sophia Thoreau (1819-1876)

the room, and, the door being opened, rushed up two
flights of stairs and leaped from the attic window to the
ice and snow by the side of the door-step, — a descent
of a little more than twenty feet, — passed round the
house and was lost. But she made her appearance again
about noon, at the window, quite well and sound in
every joint, even playful and frisky.

Journal: February 1, 1856

Min's Adventures, Part 2

Our young Maltese cat Min, which has been absent five
cold nights, the ground covered deep with crusted
snow, — her first absence — and given up for dead, has
at length returned at daylight, awakening the whole
house with her mewing and afraid of the strange girl
we have got in the meanwhile. She is a mere wrack of
skin and bones, with a sharp nose and wiry tail. She is
as one returned from the dead. There is as much rejoic-
ing as at the return of the prodigal son, and if we had a
fatted calf we should kill it. Various are the conjectures
as to her adventures, — whether she has had a fit, been
shut up somewhere, or lost, torn in pieces by a certain
terrier or frozen to death. In the meanwhile she is fed
with the best that the house affords, minced meats and
saucers of warmed milk, and, with the aid of unstinted
sleep in all laps in succession, is fast picking up her
crumbs. She has already found her old place under the
stove, and is preparing to make a stew of her brains
there.

Journal: February 28, 1856

Min's Adventures, Part 3

Sophia says that just before I came home Min caught a mouse and was playing with it in the yard. It had got away from her once or twice, and she had caught it again; and now it was stealing off again, as she lay complacently watching it with her paws tucked under her, when her friend Riordan's stout but solitary cock stepped up inquisitively, looked down at it with one eye, turning his head, then picked it up by the tail and gave it two or three whacks on the ground, and giving it a dexterous toss into the air, caught it in its open mouth, and it went head foremost and alive down his capacious throat in the twinkling of an eye, never again to be seen in this world, Min, all the while, with paws comfortably tucked under her, looking on unconcerned. What matter it one mouse more or less to her? The cock walked off amid the currant bushes, stretched his neck up, and gulped once or twice, and the deed was accomplished, and then he crowed lustily in celebration of the exploit. It might be set down among the *gesta* (if not *digesta*) *Gallorum*.[4] There were several human witnesses. It is a question whether Min ever understood where that mouse went to. Min sits composedly sentinel, with paws tucked under her, a good part of her days at present, by some ridiculous little hole, the possible entryway of a mouse. She has a habit of stretching or sharp-

---

[4] *Gesta Gallorum*: Latin, "Deeds of the Cocks." Thoreau is parodying the title of a medieval book, the *Gesta Romanorum*, or "Deeds of the Romans."

ening her claws on all smooth hair-bottomed chairs and sofas, greatly to my mother's vexation.

Journal: December 4, 1856

Frisky

A kitten is so flexible that she is almost double; the hind parts are equivalent to another kitten with which the fore part plays. She does not discover that her tail belongs to her till you tread upon it.

How eloquent she can be with her tail! Its sudden swellings and vibrations! She jumps into a chair and then stands on her hind legs to look out the window; looks steadily at objects far and near, first turning her gaze to this side then to that, for she loves to look out a window as much as any gossip. Ever and anon she bends back her ears to hear what is going on within the room, and all the while her eloquent tail is reporting the progress and success of her survey by speaking gestures which betray her interest in what she sees.

Then what a delicate hint she can give with her tail! passing perhaps underneath, as you sit at the table, and letting the tip of her tail just touch your legs, as much as to say, I am here and ready for that milk or meat, though she may not be so forward as to look round at you when she emerges.

Only skin-deep lies the feral nature of the cat, un-changed still. I just had the misfortune to rock on our cat's leg, as she was lying playfully spread out under my chair. Imagine the sound that arose, and which was excusable; but what will you say to the fierce growls and flashing eyes with which she met me for a quarter of an hour thereafter? No tiger in its jungle could have been savager.

Journal: Feburary 15, 1861

Greasy Cheeks, or: Men's Bowels

Here have been three ultra-reformers, lecturers on Slavery, Temperance, the Church, etc., in and about our house and Mrs. Brooks's the last three or four days, — A.D. Foss, once a Baptist working chaplain; and H.C. Wright, who shocks all the old women with his infidel writings. Though Foss was a stranger to the others, you would have thought them old and familiar cronies. (They happened here together by accident.) They addressed each other constantly by their Christian names, and rubbed you continually with the greasy cheeks of their kindness. They would not keep their distance, but cuddle up and lie spoon-fashion with you, no matter how hot the weather nor narrow the bed, — chiefly ——————. I was awfully pestered with this benignity; feared I should get greased all over with it past restoration; tried to keep some starch in my clothes. He wrote a book called "A Kiss for the Blow," and he behaved as if there were no alternative between these, or as if I had given him a blow. I would have preferred the blow, but he was bent on giving me the kiss, when there was neither quarrel nor agreement between us. I wanted that he should straighten his back, smooth out these ogling wrinkles of benignity about his eyes, and, with a healthy reserve, pronounce something in a downright manner. It was difficult to keep clear of his slimy benignity, with which he sought to cover you before he swallowed you and took you fairly into his bowels. It would have been far worse than the fate of Jonah. I do not wish to get any nearer to a man's bowels than usual. They lick you as a cow her calf. They would fain wrap you about with their bowels.

———————— addressed me as "Henry" within one minute from the time I first laid eyes on him, and when I spoke, he said with drawling, sultry sympathy, "Henry, I know all you would say; I understand you perfectly; you need not explain anything to me;" and to another, "I am going to dive into Henry's inmost depths." I said, "I trust you will not strike your head against the bottom." He could tell in a dark room, with his eyes blinded and in perfect stillness, if there was one there whom he loved. One of the most attractive thing about the flowers is their beautiful reserve. The truly beautiful and noble puts its lover, as it were, at an infinite distance, while it attracts him more strongly than ever. I do not like the men who come so near me with their bowels. It is the most disagreeable kind of snare to be caught in. Men's bowels are far more slimy than their brains. They must be ascetics indeed who approach you by this side.What a relief to have heard the ring of one healthy reserved tone! With such a forgiving disposition, as if he were all the while forgiving you for existing. Considering our condition or *habit* of soul, — maybe corpulent and asthmatic, — maybe dying of atrophy, with all our bones sticking out, — is it kindness to embrace a man? They lay their sweaty hand on your shoulder, or your knee, to magnetize you.

Journal: June 17, 1853

Cat Augury

The cat sleeps on her head! What does this portend?

Journal: October 1, 1858

Fire & Water

Went to a fire — or smoke — at Mrs. Hoar's. There is a slight blaze and more smoke. Two or three hundred men rush to the house, cut large holes in the roof, throw many hogsheads of water into it, — and when a few pails full well directed would suffice, — and then they run off again, leaving your attic three inches deep with water, which is rapidly descending through the ceiling to the basement and spoiling all that can be spoiled, while a torrent is running down the stairways. They were very forward to put out the fire, but they take no pains to put out the water, which does far more damage. The first was amusement; the last would be mere work and utility. Why is there not a little machine invented to throw the water out of a house?

Journal: October 10, 1860

Dumb-Bells

I see dumb-bells in the minister's study, and some of their dumbness gets into his sermons. Some travellers carry them round the world in their carpetbags. Can he be said to travel who requires still this exercise? A

party of schoolchildren had a picnic at the Easterbrooks
Country the other day, and they carried bags of beans
from their gymnasium to exercise with there. I cannot
be interested in these extremely artificial amusements.
The traveller is no longer a wayfarer, with his staff and
pack and dusty coat. He is not a pilgrim, but he travels
in a saloon, and carries dumb-bells to exercise with in
the intervals of his journey.

Journal: October 10, 1860

Did Not Promise

My Aunt Maria asked me to read the life of Dr.
Chalmers, which however I did not promise to do.
Yesterday, Sunday, she was heard through the partition
shouting to my Aunt Jane, who is deaf, "Think of it! He
stood half an hour today to hear the frogs croak, and he
wouldn't read the life of Chalmers."

Journal: March 28, 1853

Pat Haggerty's Rum

I learn that one farmer, seeing me standing a long time
still in the midst of a pool (I was watching for hylodes[5]),
said that it was his father, who had been drinking some
of Pat Haggerty's rum, and had lost his way home. So,
setting out to lead him home, he discovered that it was
I.

Journal: April 30, 1858

---

[5] A genus of frog in the Hylodidae family

Frog Dreams

I have heard now within a few days that peculiar dreaming sound of the frogs which belongs to the summer, — their midsummer night's dream. ...

The frog had eyed the heavens from his marsh, until his mind was filled with visions, and he saw more than belongs to this fenny earth. He mistrusted that he was become a dreamer and visionary. Leaping across the swamp to his fellow, what was his joy and consolation to find that he too had seen the same sights in the heavens, he too had dreamed the same dreams!

From nature we turn astonished to this *near* but supernatural fact.

Journal: May 21, 1851

Eructation

The sound of the *dreaming* frogs prevails over the others. Occasionally a bullfrog near me made an obscene noise, a sound like an eructation, near me. I think they must be imbodied eructations. They suggest flatulency.

Journal: June 13, 1851

Mephitic Bubbles

There is the faintest possible mist over the pond-holes, where the frogs are eructating, like the falling of huge drops, the bursting of mephitic air bubbles rising from the bottom, a sort of blubbering, — such conversation as I *have* heard between men, a belching conversation, expressing a sympathy of stomachs and abdomens.

Journal: July 11, 1851

Scarecrows & Pantaloons

Kings and queens who wear a suit but once, though made by some tailor or dressmaker to their majesties, cannot know the comfort of wearing a suit that fits. They are no better than wooden horses to hang the clean clothes on. Every day our garments become more assimiliated to ourselves, receiving the impress of the wearer's character, until we hesitate to lay them aside, without such delay and medical appliances and some such solemnity even as our bodies. No man ever stood the lower in my estimation for having a patch in his clothes; yet I am sure that there is greater anxiety, commonly, to have fashionable, or at least clean and unpatched clothes, than to have a sound conscience. But even if the rent is not mended, perhaps the worst vice betrayed is improvidence. I sometimes try my acquaint-ances by such tests as this; — who could wear a patch, or two extra seams only, over the knee? Most behave as if they believe that their prospects for life would be ruined if they should do it. It would be easier for them to hobble to town with a broken leg than with a broken pantaloon. Often if an accident happens to a gentle-man's legs, they can be mended; but if a similar accident happens to the legs of his pantaloons, there is no help for it; for he considers, not what is truly respectable, but what is respected. We know but few men, a great many coats and breeches. Dress a scarecrow in your last shift, you standing shiftless by, who would not soonest salute the scarecrow? Passing a cornfield the other day, close by a hat and a coat on a stake, I recognized the owner of the farm. He was only a little more weather-beaten than when I saw him last. I have heard of a dog that barked at every stranger who approached his master's premises with clothes on, but was easily quieted by a naked thief.

Walden, "Economy"

On Cape Cod, Part 2:
Dried Versus Pickled

A strict regard for truth obliges us to say that the few women whom we saw that day looked exceedingly pinched up. They had prominent chins and noses, having lost all their teeth, and a sharp *W* would represent their profile. They were not so well preserved as their husbands; or perchance they were well preserved as dried specimens. (Their husbands, however, were pickled.) But we respect them not the less for all that; our own dental system is far from perfect.

Cape Cod

Solid Bottoms

I delight to come to my bearings, — not walk in procession with pomp and parade, in a conspicuous place, but to walk even with the Builder of the universe, if I may, — not to live in this restless, nervous, bustling, trivial Nineteenth Century, but stand or sit thoughtfully while it goes by. What are men celebrating? They are all on a committee of arrangements, and hourly expect a speech from somebody. God is the only president of the day, and Webster is his orator. I love to weigh, to settle, to gravitate toward that which most strongly and rightfully attracts me; — not hang by the beam of the scale and try to weigh less, — not suppose a case, but take the case that is; to travel the only path I can, and that on which no power can resist me. It affords me no satisfaction to commence to spring an arch before I have got a solid foundation. Let us not play at kittlybenders.[6] There is a solid bottom everywhere. We read that the traveller asked the boy if the swamp before him had a solid bottom. The boy replied that it had. But presently the traveller's horse sank in up to the girths, and he observed to the boy, "I thought you said that this bog had a hard bottom." "So it has," answered the latter, "but you have not got half way to it yet." So it is with the bogs and quicksands of society; but he is an old boy that knows it.

Walden, "Conclusion"

Wages & Views

Men's minds run so much on work and money that the mass instantly associate all literary labor with a pecuniary reward. They are mainly curious to know how much money the lecturer or author gets for his work. They think that the naturalist takes so much pains to collect plants or animals because he is paid for it. An

---

[6] Kittlybenders: thin bending ice, or the act of running over such ice

Irishman who saw me in the fields making a minute in my note-book took it for granted that I was casting up my wages and actually inquired what they came to, as if he had never dreamed of any other use for writing.[7] I might have quoted to him that the wages of sin is death, as the most pertinent answer. "What do you get for lecturing now?" I am occasionally asked. It is the more amusing since I only lecture about once a year out of my native town, often not at all; so that I might as well, if my objects were merely pecuniary, give up the business. Once, when I was walking on Staten Island, looking about me as usual, a man who saw me would not believe me when I told him that I was indeed from New England but was not looking at that region with a pecuniary view, — a view to speculation; and he offered me a handsome bonus if I would sell his farm for him.

Journal: April 3, 1859

Taking Airs

I feel slightly complimented when nature condescends to make use of me without my knowledge — as when I help scatter her seeds in my walk — or carry burs and cockles on my clothes from field to field — I feel as though I had done something for the commonweal, and were entitled to board and lodging. — I take such airs upon me as the boy who holds a horse for the circus company — whom all spectators envy.

Journal: February 6, 1841

---

[7] See also the essay "Getting a Living" at the end of this book.

How to Clear a Field

Grasshoppers have been very abundant in dry fields for
two or three weeks. Sophia walked through the Depot
field a fortnight ago, and when she got home picked
fifty or sixty from her skirts, — for she wore hoops and
crinoline. Would not this be a good way to clear a field
of them, — to send a bevy of fashionably dressed ladies
across a field and leave them to clean their skirts when
they got home? It would supplant anything at the
patent office, and the motive power is cheap.

Journal: September 16, 1859

For a Dollar

Formerly, when how to get my living honestly, with
freedom left for my proper pursuits, was a question
which vexed me even more than it does now, for
unfortunately I am become somewhat callous, I used to
see a large box by the railroad, six feet long by three
wide, in which the laborers locked up their tools at
night, and it suggested to me that every man who was
hard-pushed might get such a one for a dollar, and,
having bored a few auger holes in it, to admit the air at
least, get into it when it rained and at night, and hook
down the lid, and so have freedom in his love, and in his
soul be free. This does not appear the worst, nor by any
means a despicable alternative. You could sit up as late
as you pleased, and, whenever you got up, go abroad
without any landlord or house-lord dogging you for
rent. Many a man is harassed to death to pay the rent of

a larger and more luxurious box who would not have frozen to death in such a box as this.

Walden, "Economy"

Do Not Nip Me in a Vital Part

I think that a man is at a dead set who has got through a knot hole or gateway where his sledgeload of furniture cannot follow him. I cannot but feel compassion when I hear some trig, compact-looking man, seemingly free, all girded and ready, speak of his "furniture," as whether it is insured or not. "But what shall I do with my furniture?" My gay butterfly is entangled in a spider's web then. Even those who seem for a long while not to have any, if you inquire more narrowly you find have some stored in somebody's barn. I look upon England today as an old gentleman who is travelling with a great deal of baggage, trumpery which has accumulated from long housekeeping, which he has not the courage to burn; great trunk, little trunk, bandbox and bundle. Throw away the first three at least. It would surpass the powers of a well man nowadays to take up his bed and walk, and I should certainly advise a sick one to lay down his bed and run. When I have met an immigrant tottering under a bundle which contained his all — looking like an enormous wen which had grown out of the nape of his neck — I have pitied him, not because that was his all, but because he had all *that* to carry. If I have got to drag my trap, I will take care that it be a light one and do not nip me in a vital part.

But perchance it would be wisest to never put one's paw
into it.

Walden, "Economy"

The Next Hundred Dollars

Within the last five years I have had the command of a
little more money than in the previous five years, for I
have sold some books and some lectures; yet I have not
been a whit better fed or clothed or warmed or shel-
tered, not a whit richer, except that I have been less
concerned about my living, but perhaps my life has
been the less serious for it, and, to balance it, I feel now
that there is a possibility of failure. Who knows but I
may come upon the town, if, as is likely, the public want
no more of my books, or lectures (which last is already
the case)? Before, I was much likelier to take the town
upon my shoulders. That is, I have lost some of my
independence on them, when they would say that I had
gained an independence. If you wish to give a man a
sense of poverty, give him a thousand dollars. The next
hundred dollars he gets will not be worth more than
ten that he used to get. Have pity on him; withhold
your gifts.

Journal: January 20, 1856

The Poorer I Am

What you call bareness and poverty is to me simplicity.
God could not be unkind to me if he should try. I love
the winter, with its imprisonment and its cold, for it
compels the prisoner to try new fields and resources. I

love best to have each thing in its season only, and enjoy doing without it at all other times. It is the greatest of all advantages to enjoy no advantage at all. I find it invariably true, the poorer I am, the richer I am. I have never got over my surprise that I should have been born into the most estimable place in all the world, and in the very nick of time, too.

Journal: December 5, 1856

Disappointing Dollars

Again and again I congratulate myself on my so-called poverty. I was almost disappointed yesterday to find thirty dollars in my desk which I did not know that I possessed, though now I should be sorry to lose it.

Journal: February 8, 1857

Nine Hundred Volumes

For a year or two past, my *publisher*, falsely so called, has been writing from time to time to ask what disposition should be made of the copies of "A Week on the Concord and Merrimack Rivers"[8] still on hand, and at last suggesting that he had use for the room they occupied in his cellar. So I had them all sent to me here, and they have arrived today by express, filling the man's wagon, — 706 copies out of an edition of 1000 which I bought of Munroe four years ago and have been ever

---

[8] Thoreau's first book. Though he first sought a publisher in 1847, the book did not appear until May 30, 1849, under a deal in which the author guaranteed to cover production costs if it did not sell.

since paying for, and have not quite paid yet. The wares are sent to me at last, and I have an opportunity to examine my purchase. They are something more substantial than fame, as my back knows, which has borne them up two flights of stairs to a place similar to that to which they trace their origin. Of the remaining two hundred and ninety odd, seventy-five were given away, the rest sold. I have now a library of nearly nine hundred volumes, over seven hundred of which I wrote myself. Is it not well that the author should behold the fruits of his labor? My works are piled up on one side of my chamber half as high as my head, my *opera omnia*. This is authorship; these are the work of my brain. There was just one piece of good luck in the venture. The unbound were tied up by the printer four years ago in stout paper wrappers, and inscribed —

H. D. THOREAU'S
CONCORD RIVER
50 COPS.

So Munroe had only to cross out "River" and write "Mass." and deliver them to the expressman at once. I can see now what I write for, the result of my labors.

Nevertheless, in spite of this result, sitting beside the inert mass of my works, I take up my pen tonight to record what thought or experience I may have had, with as much satisfaction as ever. Indeed, I believe that this result is more inspiring and better for me than if a thousand had bought my wares. It affects my privacy less and leaves me freer.

Journal: October 28, 1854

Best Dressed

I had a suit once in which, methinks, I could glide across the fields unperceived half a mile in front of a farmer's windows. It was such a skillful mixture of browns, dark and light properly proportioned, with even some threads of green in it by chance. It was of loose texture and about the color of a pasture with patches of withered sweet-fern and lechea. I trusted a good deal to my invisibility in it when going across lots, and many a time I was aware that to it I owed the near approach of wild animals.

No doubt my dusty and tawny cowhides surprise the street walkers who wear patent leather or Congress shoes, but they do not consider how absurd such shoes would be in my vocation, to thread the woods and swamps in. Why should I wear *Congress* who walk alone, and not where there is any congress of my kind?

Channing[9] was saying, properly enough, the other day, as we were making our way through a dense patch of shrub oak: "I suppose that those villagers think that we wear these old and worn hats with holes all along the corners for oddity, but Coombs, the musquash hunter and partridge and rabbit snarer, knows better.

---

[9] William Ellery Channing, a Concord resident and best friend of Thoreau

He understands us. He knows that new and square-cornered hat would be spoiled in one excursion through shrub oaks."

The walker and naturalist does not wear a hat, or a shoe, or a coat, to be looked at, but for other uses. When a citizen comes to take a walk with me I commonly find that he is lame, — disabled by his shoeing. He is sure to wet his feet, tear his coat, and jam his hat, and the superior qualities of my boots, coat, and hat appear. I once went into the woods with a party for a fortnight. I wore my old and common clothes, which were of Vermont gray. They wore, no doubt, the best they had for such an occasion, — of a fashionable color and quality. I thought that they were a little ashamed of me while we were in the towns. They all tore their clothes badly but myself, and I, who, it chanced, was the only one provided with needles and thread, enabled them to mend them. When we came out of the woods I was the best dressed of any of them.

Journal: March 26, 1860

Fox Skating

Yesterday I skated after a fox over the ice. Occasionally he sat on his haunches and barked at me like a young wolf. ...

All brutes seem to have a genius for mystery — an oriental aptitude for symbols and the language of signs. ... The fox manifested an almost human suspicion of mystery in my actions. While I skated directly after him, he cantered at the top of his speed, but when I stood still, though his fear was not abated some strange but inflexible law of his nature caused him to stop also, and sit again on his haunches. While I stood motionless, he would go slowly a rod to one side, then sit and bark, then a rod to the other side, and sit and bark again, but did not retreat, as if spell-bound. When however I commenced the pursuit again he found himself released from his durance.

Journal: undated (1842-44)

Skating Fast, Part 1

Skated to Baker Farm with a rapidity which astonished myself, before the wind, feeling the rise and fall, — the water having settled in the suddenly cold night, — which I had not time to see. A man feels like a new creature, a deer, perhaps, moving at this rate. He takes new possession of nature in the name of his own majesty. There was I, and there, and there, as Mercury went down the Idaean Mountains.

Journal: January 14, 1855

Skating Fast, Part 2

P.M.—Skated to Bedford

It had just been snowing, and this lay in shallow drifts or waves on the Great Meadows, alternate snow and ice. Skated into a crack, and slid on my side twenty-five feet.

Journal: January 15, 1855

Skating Fast, Part 3

Wednesday.

A clear, cold, beautiful day. Fine skating, and unprece-dented expanse of ice. ... It was quite an adventure get-ting over the bridgeways or causeways, for on every shore there was either water or thin ice which would not bear. ... You were often liable to be thrown when skating fast, by the shallow puddles on the ice formed in the middle of the day and not easy to be distinguished. These detained your feet while your unimpeded body fell forward. ...

Journal: January 31, 1855

Skating Fast, Part 4

Snowed again half an inch more in the evening, after which, at ten o'clock, the moon still obscured, I skated on the river and meadows. Our skates make but little sound in this coating of snow about an inch thick, as if we had on woollen skates, and we can easily see our tracks in the night. We seem thus to go faster than before by day, not only because we do not see (but feel and imagine) our rapidity, but because of the impression which the mysterious muffled sound of our feet makes. Now and then we skated into some chippy, crackling white ice, where a superficial puddle had run dry before freezing hard, and got a tumble.

Journal: February 2, 1855

Skating Fast, Part 5

This morning it is snowing again. This will deserve to be called the winter of skating.

Skated up the river with Tappan in spite of the snow and wind. It was a novel experience, this skating through snow, sometimes a mile without a bare spot, this blustering day. In many places a crack ran across our course where the water had oozed out, and the driving snow catching in it had formed a thick batter with a stiffish crust in which we were tripped up and measured our lengths on the ice. The few thin places were concealed, and we avoided them by our knowledge of the localities. Sometimes a thicker drift, too, threw us, or a sudden unevenness in the concealed ice; but on the whole the snow was but a slight obstruction. We skated with much more facility than I had anticipated, and I would not have missed the experience for a good deal.

We went up the Pantry Meadow above the old William Wheeler house, and came down this meadow again with the wind and snow dust, spreading our coat-tails, like birds, though somewhat at the risk of our necks if we had struck a foul place. I found that I could sail on a tack pretty well, trimming with my skirts. Sometimes we had to jump suddenly over some obstacle which the snow had concealed before, to save our necks. It was worth the while for one to look back against the sun and wind and see the other sixty rods off coming, floating down like a graceful demon in the midst of the broad meadow all covered and lit with the curling snow-steam, between which you saw the ice in dark, waving streaks, like a mighty river Orellana[10] braided of a myriad steaming currents, — like the demon of the storm driving his flocks and herds before him. In the midst of this tide of curling snow-steam, he sweeps and surges this way and that and comes on like the spirit of the whirlwind.

Journal: February 3, 1855

Skating Fast, Part 6

I think more of skates than of the horse or locomotive as annihilators of distance, for while I am getting along with the speed of the horse, I have at the same time the satisfaction of the horse and his rider, and far more adventure and variety than if I were riding. We never cease to be surprised when we observe how swiftly the skater glides along. Just compare him with one walking or running. The walker is but a snail in comparison, and the runner gives up the contest after a few rods. The skater can afford to follow all the windings of the stream, and yet soon leaves far behind and out of sight the walker who cuts across. Distance is hardly an obstacle to him. … The briskest walkers appear to be stationary to the skater. The skater has wings, *talaria*, to his feet. Moreover, you have such perfect control of your feet that you can take advatange of the narrowest and most winding and sloping bridge of ice in order to

---

[10] The Amazon River, first explored by Europeans under Francisco de Orellana in 1541

pass between the button-bushes and the open stream or under a bridge on a narrow shelf, where the walker cannot go at all. You can glide securely within an inch of destruction on this the most slippery of surfaces, more securely than you could walk there, perhaps, on any other material. You can pursue swiftly the most intricate and winding path, even leaping obstacles which suddenly present themselves.

Journal: December 29, 1858

Weighty Argument

The other day, as I stood on Walden, drinking at a puddle on the ice, which was probably two feet thick, and thinking how lucky I was that I had not got to cut through all that thickness, I was amused to see an Irish laborer on the railroad, who had come down to drink, timidly tiptoeing toward me in his cowhide boots, lifting them nearly two feet at each step and fairly trembling with fear, as if the ice were already bending beneath his ponderous body and he were about to be engulfed. "Why, my man," I called out to him, "this ice will bear a loaded train, half a dozen locomotives side by side, a whole herd of oxen," suggesting whatever would be a weighty argument with him. And so at last he fairly straightened up and quenched his thirst. It was very ludicrous to me, who was thinking, by chance, what a labor it would be to get at the water with an axe there and that I was lucky to find some on the surface.

So, when I have been resting and quenching my thirst on the eternal plains of truth, where rests the base of those beautiful columns that sustain the heavens, I have been amused to see a traveler who had long confined himself to the quaking shore, which was all covered with the traces of the deluge, come timidly tiptoeing toward me, trembling in every limb.

Journal: February 4, 1857

Bedlam

They tell how I swung on a gown on the stairway when I was at Chelmsford. The gown gave way; I fell and fainted, and it took two pails of water to bring me to, for I was remarkable for holding my breath in those cases.

Mother tried to milk the cow which Father took on trial, but she kicked at her and spilt the milk. (They say a dog had bitten her teats.) Proctor laughed at her as a city girl, and then he tried, but the cow kicked him over, and he finished by beating her with his cowhide shoe. Captain Richardson milked her warily, standing up. Father came home, and thought he would "bustle right up to her," for she needed much to be milked, but suddenly, she lifted her leg and "struck him fair and square in the muns," knocked him flat, and broke the bridge of his nose, which shows it yet. He distinctly heard her hoof rattle on his nose. This "started the claret," and, without stanching the blood, he at once drove her home to the man he had her of. She ran at some young women by the way, who saved themselves by getting over the wall in haste.

Father complained of the powder in the meeting-house garret at town meeting, but it did not get moved while we lived there. Here he painted over his old signs for guide-boards, and got a fall when painting Hale's factory. Here the bladder John[11] was playing with burst on the hearth. The cow came into the entry after pumpkins. I cut my toe, and was knocked over by a hen with chickens, etc., etc.

Mother tells how, at the brick house, we each had a little garden a few feet square, and I came in one day, having found a potato just sprouted, which by her advice I planted in my garden. Ere long John came in with a potato which he had found and had it planted in his garden, — "Oh, mother, I have found a potato all sprouted. I mean to put it in my garden," etc. Even Helen[12] is said to have found one. But next I came crying that somebody had got my potato, etc., etc., but it was restored to me as the youngest and original discoverer, if not inventor, of the potato, and it grew in *my* garden, and finally its crop was dug by myself and yielded a dinner for the family.

I was kicked down by a passing ox. Had a chicken given me by Lidy — Hannah — and peeped through the keyhole at it. Caught an eel with John. Went to bed with new boots on, and after with cap. "Rasselas" given me, etc., etc. Asked P. Wheeler, "Who owns all the land?" Asked Mother, having got the medal for

---

[11] Henry's older brother John Thoreau (1815-1842)
[12] Henry's older sister Helen Thoreau (1812-1849)

geography, "Is Boston in Concord?"

Journal: January 7, 1856

My Uncle Charles

People are talking about my Uncle Charles. Minott tells how he heard Tilly Brown once asking him to show him a peculiar (inside?) lock in wrestling. "Now, don't hurt me, don't throw me hard." He struck his antagonist inside his knees with his feet, and so deprived him of his legs. Hosmer remembers his tricks in the barroom, shuffling cards, etc. He could do anything with cards, yet he did not gamble. He would toss up his hat, twirling it over and over, and catch it on his head invariably. Once wanted to live at Hosmer's, but the latter was afraid of him. "Can't we study up something?" he asked. H. asked him into the house and brought out apples and cider, and Charles talked. "You!" said he, "I burst the bully of Lowell" (or Haverhill?). He wanted to wrestle; would not be put off. "Well, we won't wrestle in the house." So they went out to the yard, and a crowd got round. "Come spread some straw here," said C. "I don't want to hurt him." He threw him at once. They tried again. He told them to spread more straw and he "burst" him.

He had a strong head and never got drunk; would drink sometimes, but not to excess. Did not use tobacco, except snuff out of another's box sometimes. Was very neat in his person. Was not profane, though vulgar. ...

Uncle Charles used to say that he had n't a single tooth in his head. The fact was they were all double, and I have heard that he lost about all of them by the time he was twenty-one. Ever since I knew him he could swallow his nose.

Journal: April 30, 1856

My Uncle Charles, Again

E. Hosmer says that a man told him that he had seen my uncle Charles take a twelve-foot ladder, set it up straight, and then run up and down the other side, kicking it from behind him as he went down.

Journal: March 11, 1859

Dust

Sophia says, bringing company into my sanctum, by way of apology, that I regard the dust on my furniture like the bloom on fruits, not to be swept off.

Journal: September 15, 1856

Pen & Pendulum

Time never passes so quickly and unaccountably as when I am engaged in composition, *i.e.* in writing down my thoughts. Clocks seem to have been put forward.

Journal: January 27, 1858

Chickening

When the poetic frenzy seizes us, we run and scratch with our pen, delighting, like a cock, in the dust we make, but do not detect where the jewel lies, which perhaps we have in the meantime cast at a distance, or quite covered up again.

Journal: February 8, 1839

Hen Head

"As fat as a hen in the forehead," — a saying which I heard my father use this morning.

Journal: February 21, 1852

Prick Himself

How protean is life! One may eat and drink and sleep and digest, and do the ordinary duties of man, and have no excuse for sending for a doctor, and yet he may have reason to doubt if he is as truly alive or his life is as valuable and divine as that of an oyster. He may be the very best citizen in the town, and yet it shall occur to him to prick himself with a pin to see if he is alive. It is wonderful how quiet, harmless, and ineffective a living creature may be. No more energy may it have than a fungus that lifts the bark of a decaying tree.

Journal: January 26, 1858

Dissolved

Drifting in a sultry day on the sluggish waters of the pond, I almost cease to live and begin to be. A boatman stretched on the deck of his craft and dallying with the noon would be as apt an emblem of eternity for me as the serpent with the tail in his mouth. I am never so prone to lose my identity. I am dissolved in the haze.

Journal: April 1838

Whistle

The golden robin keeps whistling something like *Eat it, Potter, eat it!*

Journal: May 25, 1855

Henry & Chuck

As I turned round the corner of Hubbard's Grove, saw a woodchuck, the first of the season, in the middle of the field, six or seven rods from the fence which bounds the wood, and twenty rods distant. I ran along the fence and cut him off, or rather overtook him, though he started at the same time. When I was only a rod and a half off, he stopped, and I did the same; then he ran again, and I ran up within three feet of him, when he stopped again, the fence being between us. I squatted down and surveyed him at my leisure. His eyes were dull black and rather inobvious, with a faint chestnut (?) iris, but with little expression and that more of resignation than of anger. The general aspect was a coarse grayish brown, a sort of grisel (?). A lighter brown next the skin, then black or very dark brown and tipped with whitish rather loosely. The head between a squirrel and a bear, flat on the top and dark brown, and darker still or black on the tip of the nose. The whiskers black, two inches long. The ears very small and roundish, set far back and nearly buried in the fur. Black feet, with long and slender claws for digging. It appeared to tremble, or perchance shivered with cold. When I moved, it gritted its teeth quite loud, sometimes striking the underjaw against the other chatteringly, sometimes grinding one jaw on the other, yet as if more from instinct than anger. Whichever way I turned, that way it headed. I took a twig a foot long and touched its snout, at which it started forward and bit the stick, lessening the distance between us to two feet, and still it held all the ground it gained. I played with it tenderly awhile with the stick, trying to open its gritting jaws. Ever its long incisors, two above and two below, were presented. But I thought it would go to sleep if I stayed long enough. It did not sit upright as sometimes, but *standing* on its forefeet with its head down; *i.e.* half sitting, half standing. We sat looking at one another about half an hour, till we began to feel mesmeric influences. When I was tired, I moved away, wishing to see him run, but I could not start him. I walked round him; he turned as fast and fronted me still. I sat down by his side within a foot. I talked to him *quasi* forest lingo, baby-talk, at any rate in a conciliatory tone, and thought that I had some influence on him. He gritted his teeth less. I chewed checkerberry leaves and presented them to his nose at last without a grit; though I saw that by so much gritting of the teeth he had worn them rapidly and they were covered with a fine white powder, which, if you measured it thus, would have made his anger terrible. He did not mind any noise I might make. With a little stick I lifted one of his paws to examine it, and held it up at pleasure. I turned him over to see what color he was beneath (darker or more purely brown), though he turned himself back again sooner than I could have wished. His tail was also all brown, though not very dark, rat-tail like, with loose hairs standing out on all sides like a caterpillar brush. He had a rather mild look. I spoke kindly to him. I reached checkerberry leaves to his mouth. I stretched my hands over him, though he turned up his head and still gritted a little. I laid my hand on him, but immediately took it off again, instinct not being wholly overcome. If I had had a few fresh bean leaves, thus in advance of the season, I am sure I should have tamed him completely. It was a frizzly tail. His is a humble, terrestrial color like a partridge's, well-concealed where dead wiry grass rises above darker brown or chestnut dead leaves, — a modest color. If I had had some food, I should have ended with stroking him at my leisure. Could easily have wrapped him in my handkerchief. He was not fat nor particularly lean. I finally had to leave him without seeing him move from the place. A large, clumsy, burrowing squirrel. *Arctomys,* bear-mouse. I respect him as one of the natives. He lies there, by his color and habits so naturalized amid the dry leaves, the withered grass, and the bushes. A sound nap, too, he has enjoyed in his native fields, the past winter. I think I might learn some wisdom of him. His ancestors have lived here longer than mine.

Journal: April 16, 1852

Entrance to the Oracle

Verily I am the creature of circumstances. Here I have swallowed an indispensable tooth, and so am no whole man, but a lame and halting piece of manhood. I am conscious of no gap in my soul, but it would seem that, now the entrance to the oracle has been enlarged, the more rare and commonplace the responses that issue from it. I have felt cheap, and hardly dared hold up my head among men, ever since this accident happened. Nothing can I do as well and freely as before; nothing do I undertake but I am hindered and balked by this circumstance. Virtue and Triumph go undefended, and Falsehood and Affectation are thrown in my teeth, — though I am toothless. But let the lame man shake his leg, and match himself with the fleetest in the race. So shall he do what is in him to do. But let him who has lost a tooth open his mouth wide and gabble, lisp, and sputter never so resolutely.

Journal: August 27, 1838

Lip Greediness

Old Cato says well, "*Patremfamilias vendacem, non emacem, esse oportet.*"[13] These Latin terminations express better than any English that I know the greediness, as it were, and tenacity of purpose with which the husbandman and householder is required to be a seller and not a buyer, — with mastiff-like tenacity, — these *lipped* words, which, like the lips of moose and browsing creatures, gather in the herbage and twigs with a certain greed. This termination *cious* adds force to a word, like the lips of browsing creatures, which

---

[13] "The head of the family should be eager to sell, not to buy." From Cato's *De Agricultura.*

greedily collect what the jaw holds; as in the word "tenacious" the first half represents the kind of jaw which holds, the last the lips which collect. It can only be pronounced by a certain opening and protruding of the lips; so "avaricious." These words express the sense of their simple roots with the addition, as it were, of a certain lip greediness. Hence "capacious" and "capacity," "emacity." When these expressive words are used, the hearer gets something to chew upon. What is *luscious* is especially enjoyed by the lips. To be edacious and voracious is to be not nibbling and swallowing merely, but eating and swallowing while the lips are greedily collecting more food.

There is a reptile in the throat of the greedy man always thirsting and famishing. It is not his own natural hunger and thirst which he satisfies.

Journal: September 2, 1851

The Snake in My Stomach

How can that depth be fathomed where a man will see himself reflected? The rill I stopped to drink at I drink in more than I expected. … I do not drink in vain. I mark that brook as if I had swallowed a water snake that would live in my stomach. I have swallowed something worth the while. The day is not what it was before I stooped to drink. Ah, I shall hear from that draught! It is not in vain that I have drunk. I have drunk an arrowhead. It flows from where all fountains rise.

How many ova have I swallowed? Who knows

77

what will be hatched within me? There were some seeds of thought, methinks, floating in that water, which are expanding in me. The man must not drink of the running streams, the living waters, who is not prepared to have all nature reborn in him, — to suckle monsters. The snake in my stomach lifts his head to my mouth at the sound of running water. When was it that I swallowed the snake? I have got rid of the snake in my stomach. I drank of stagnant waters once. That accounts for it. I caught him by the throat and drew him out, and had a well day after all. Is there not such a thing as getting rid of the snake which you have swallowed when young, when thoughtless you stooped and drank at stagnant waters, which has worried you in your waking hours and in your sleep ever since, and appropriated the life that was yours? Will he not ascend into your mouth at the sound of running water? Then catch him boldly by the head and draw him out, though you may think his tail be curled about your vitals.

Journal: August 17, 1851

Went to a Party

In the evening went to a party. It is a bad place to go to, — thirty or forty persons, mostly young women, in a small room, warm and noisy. Was introduced to two young women. The first one was as lively and loquacious as a chickadee; had been accustomed to the society of watering places, and therefore could get no refreshment out of such a dry fellow as I. The other was said to be pretty looking, but I rarely look people in their faces, and, moreover, I could not hear what she said, there was such a clacking, — could only see the motion of her lips when I looked that way. I could imagine better places for conversation, where there should be a certain degree of silence surrounding you, and less than forty talking at once. Why, this afternoon, even, I did better. There was old Mr. Joseph Hosmer and I ate our luncheon [sic] of cracker and cheese together in the woods. I heard all he said, though it was not much, to be sure, and he could hear me. And then he talked out of such a glorious repose, taking a leisurely bite at the cracker and cheese between his words; and so some of him was communicated to me, and some of me to him, I trust.

These parties, I think, are a part of the machinery of modern society, that young people may be brought together to form marriage connections.

What is the use of going to see people whom yet you never see, and who never see you? I begin to suspect that it is not necessary that we should see one another.

Journal: November 14, 1851

Scamp

My *Journal* should be the record of my love. I would write in it only of the things I love, my affection for any aspect of the world, what I love to think of. I have no more distinctness or pointedness in my yearnings than an expanding bud, which does indeed point to flower and fruit, to summer and autumn, but is aware of the warm sun and spring influence only. I feel ripe for something, yet do nothing, can't discover what that thing is. I feel fertile merely. It is seedtime with me. I have lain fallow long enough.

Notwithstanding a sense of unworthiness which possesses me, not without reason, notwithstanding that I regard myself as a good deal of a scamp, yet for the most part the spirit of the universe is unnacountably kind to me, and I enjoy perhaps an unusual share of happiness. Yet I question sometimes if there is not some settlement to come.

Journal: November 16, 1850

Alcott's Venison

Alcott[14] spent the day with me yesterday. He spent the day before with Emerson. He observed that he had got his wine and now he had come after his venison. Such was the compliment he paid me.

Journal: August 10, 1853

Never Got Audited

For a long time I was reporter to a journal, of no very wide circulation, whose editor has never yet seen fit to print the bulk of my contributions,[15] and, as is too common with writers, I got only my labor for my pains. However, in this case my pains were their own reward.

---

[14] Amos Bronson Alcott (1799-1888), father of Louisa May Alcott, was a teacher, writer, and Transcendentalist.
[15] Thoreau is referring to his own private journal, of which he is both writer and editor.

For many years I was self-appointed inspector of snow storms and rain storms, and did my duty faithfully; surveyor, if not of highways, then of forest paths and all across-lot routes, keeping them open, and ravines bridged and passable at all seasons, where the public heel had testified to their utility.[16]

I have looked after the wild stock of the town, which give a faithful herdsman a good deal of trouble by leaping fences; and I have had an eye to the unfrequented nooks and corners of the farm; though I did not always know whether Jonas or Solomon worked in a particular field today; that was none of my business. I have watered the red huckleberry, the sand cherry and the nettle tree, the red pine and the black ash, the white grape and the yellow violet, which might have withered else in dry seasons.[17]

In short, I went on thus for a long time, I may say it without boasting, faithfully minding my business, till it became more and more evident that my townsmen would not after all admit me into the list of town officers. My accounts, which I can swear to have kept faithfully, I have, indeed, never got audited, still less accepted, still less paid and settled. However, I have not set my heart on that.

Walden, "Economy"

---

[16] Thoreau was an inveterate trespasser, liberally crossing private properties in his exploration of the natural life around Concord.

[17] i.e., Thoreau has peed on all these flora.

Loon Checkers

As I was paddling along the north shore one very calm
October afternoon, for such days especially they settle
onto the lakes, like the milkweed down, having looked
in vain over the pond for a loon, suddenly one, sailing
out from the shore toward the middle a few rods in
front of me, set up his wild laugh and betrayed himself.
I pursued with a paddle and he dived, but when he came
up I was nearer than before. He dived again, but I mis-
calculated the direction he would take, and we were
fifty rods apart when he came to the surface this time,
for I had helped to widen the interval; and again he
laughed long and loud, and with more reason than
before. He maneuvered so cunningly that I could not
get within half a dozen rods of him. Each time, when he
came to the surface, turning his head this way and that,
he coolly surveyed the water and the land, and apparently chose his course so that he might come up where
there was the widest expanse of water and at the greatest distance from the boat. It was surprising how quickly he made up his mind and put his resolve into execution. He led me at once to the widest part of the pond,
and could not be driven from it. While he was thinking
one thing in his brain, I was endeavoring to divine his
thought in mine. It was a pretty game, played on the
smooth surface of the pond, a man against a loon. Suddenly your adversary's checker disappears beneath the
board, and the problem is to place yours nearest to
where his will appear again. Sometimes he would come
up unexpectedly on the opposite side of me, having

apparently passed directly under the boat. So long-winded was he and so unweariable, that when he had swum farthest he would immediately plunge again, nevertheless; and then no wit could divine where in the deep pond, beneath the smooth surface, he might be speeding his way like a fish, for he had time and ability to visit the bottom of the pond in its deepest part. It is said that loons have been caught in the New York lakes eighty feet beneath the surface, with hooks set for trout, — though Walden is deeper than that. How surprised must the fishes be to see this ungainly visitor from another sphere speeding his way amid their schools! Yet he appeared to know his course as surely under the water as on the surface, and swam much faster there. Once or twice I saw a ripple where he approached the surface, just put his head out to reconnoitre, and instantly dived again. I found that it was as well for me to rest on my oars and wait his reappearing as to endeavor to calculate where he would rise; for again and again, when I was straining my eyes over the surface one way, I would suddenly be startled by his unearthly laugh behind me. But why, after displaying so much cunning, did he invariably betray himself the moment he came up by that loud laugh? Did not his white breast enough betray him? He was indeed a silly loon, I thought. I could commonly hear the plash of the water when he came up, and so also detected him. But after an hour he seemed as fresh as ever, dived as willingly and swam yet farther than at first. It was surprising to see how serenely he sailed off with unruffled breast when he came to the surface, doing all the work with his webbed feet beneath. His usual note was this demoniac laughter, yet somewhat like that of a water-fowl; but occasionally, when he had balked me most successfully and come up a long way off, he uttered a long-drawn unearthly howl, probably more like that of a wolf than any bird; as when a beast puts his muzzle to the ground and deliberately howls. This was his looning, — perhaps the wildest sound that is ever heard here, making the woods ring far and wide. I concluded that he laughed in derision of my efforts, confident of his own resources. Though the sky was by this time overcast, the pond was so smooth that I could see where he broke the surface when I did not hear him. His white breast, the stillness of the air, and the smoothness of the water were all against him. At length, having come up fifty rods off, he uttered one of those prolonged howls, as if calling on the god of loons to aid him, and immediately there came a wind from the east and rippled the surface, and filled the whole air with misty rain, and I was impressed as if it were the prayer of the loon answered, and his god was angry with me; and so I left him disappearing far away on the tumultuous surface.

Walden, "Brute Neighbors"

Fox Chase

Suddenly, looking down the river, I saw a fox some sixty rods off, making across the hills on my left. As the snow lay five inches deep, he made but slow progress, but it was no impediement to me. So, yielding to the instinct of the chase, I tossed my head aloft and bounded away, snuffing the air like a fox-hound, and spurning the world and the Humane Society at each bound. It seemed the woods rang with the hunter's horn, and Diana and all the satyrs joined in the chase and cheered me on. Olympian and Elean youths were waving palms on the hills. In the meanwhile I gained rapidly on the fox; but he showed a remarkable presence of mind, for, instead of keeping up the face of the hill, which was steep and unwooded in that part, he kept along the slope in the direction of the forest, though he lost ground by it. Notwithstanding his fright, he took no step which was not beautiful. The course on his part was a series of most graceful curves. It was a sort of leopard canter, I should say, as if he were nowise impeded by the snow, but were husbanding his strength all the while. When he doubled I wheeled and cut him off, bounding with fresh vigor, and Antaeus-like, recovering my strength each time I touched the snow.[18] Having got near enough for a fair view, just as he was slipping into the wood, I gracefully yielded him the palm. He ran as though there were not a bone in his back, occasionally dropping his muzzle to the snow for a rod or two, and then tossing his head aloft when satisfied of his course. When he came to a declivity he put his forefeet together and slid down it like a cat. He trod so softly that you could not have

***

[18] The Greek god Antaeus drew strength from touching the earth, which was his mother Gaea.

heard it from any nearness, and yet with such expression that it would not have been quite inaudible at any distance. So, hoping this experience would prove a useful lesson to him, I returned to the village by the highway of the river.

Journal: January 30, 1841

Squirreling

I hear the alarum of a small red squirrel. I see him running by fits and starts along a chestnut bough toward me. His head looks disproportionately large for his body, like a bulldog's, perhaps because he has his chaps full of nuts. He chirrups and vibrates his tail, holds himself in, and scratches along a foot as if it were a mile. He finds noise and activity for both of us. It is evident that all this ado does not proceed from fear. There is at the bottom, no doubt, an excess of inquisitiveness and caution, but the greater part is make-believe, and a love of the marvelous. He can hardly keep it up till I am gone, however, but takes out his nut and tastes it in the midst of his agitation. *"See there, see there,"* says he, "who's that? O dear, what shall I do?" and makes believe run off, but does n't get along an inch, — lets it all pass off by flashes through his tail, while he clings to the bark as if he were holding in a race-horse. He gets down the trunk at last on to a projecting knot, head downward, within a rod of you, and chirrups and chatters louder than ever. Tries to work himself into a fright. The hind part of his body is urging the forward part along, snapping the tail over it like a whip-lash, but the fore part, for the most part, clings fast to the bark with desperate energy. *Squirr*, "to throw with a jerk," seems to have quite as much to do with the name as the Greek *skia oura*, shadow and tail.

Journal: October 5, 1857

Bird Clockwork

Jacob Farmer tells me that one Sunday he went to his barn, having nothing to do, and thought he would watch the swallows, republican swallows. The old bird was feeding her young, and he sat within fifteen feet, overlooking them. There were five young, and he was curious to know how each received its share; and as often as the bird came with a fly, the one at the door (or opening) took it, and then they all hitched round one notch, so that a new one was presented at the door, who received the next fly; and this was the invariable order, the same one never receiving two flies in succession. At last the old bird brought a very small fly, and the young one that swallowed it did not desert his ground but waited to receive the next, but when the bird came with another, of the usual size, she commenced a loud and long scolding at the little one, till it resigned its place, and the next in succession received the fly.

Journal: November 9, 1857

Wild Mice

The mice which haunted my house were not the common ones, which are said to have been introduced into the country, but a wild native kind not found in the village. I sent one to a distinguished naturalist, and it interested him much. When I was building, one of these had its nest underneath the house, and before I had lain the second floor, and swept out the shavings, would come out regularly at lunch time and pick up the crumbs at my feet. It probably had never seen a man before; and it soon became quite familiar, and would run over my shoes and up my clothes. It could readily ascend the sides of the room by short impulses, like a squirrel, which it resembled in its motions. As length, as I leaned with my elbow on the bench one day, it ran up my clothes, and along my sleeve, and round and round the paper which held my dinner, while I kept the latter close, and dodged and played at bo-peep with it; and when at last I still held a piece of cheese between my thumb and finger, it came and nibbled it, sitting in my hand, and afterward cleaned its face and paws, like a fly, and walked away.

Walden, "Brute Neighbors"

Inconvenience

One inconvenience I sometimes experienced in so small a house,[19] the difficulty of getting to a sufficient dist-ance from my guest when we began to utter the big thoughts in big words. You want room for your thoughts to get into sailing trim and run a course or two before they make their port. The bullet of your

---

[19]Thoreau's house at Walden measured 10 feet by 15 feet, with an 8-foot ceiling.

thoughts must have overcome its lateral and ricochet motion and fallen into its last and steady course before it reaches the ear of the hearer, else it may plough out again through the side of his head. Also, our sentences wanted room to unfold and form their columns in the interval. Individuals, like nations, must have broad and natural boundaries, even a considerable neutral ground between them. I have found it a singular luxury to talk across the pond to a companion on the opposite side. In my house we were so near that we could not begin to hear, — we could not speak low enough to be heard; as when you throw two stones into a calm water so near that they break each other's undulations. If we are merely loqacious and loud talkers, then we can afford to stand very near together, cheek by jowl, and feel each other's breath; but if we speak reservedly and thought-fully, we want to be farther apart, that all animal heat and moisture may have a chance to evaporate. If we would enjoy the most intimate society with that in each of us which is without, or above, being spoken to, we must not only be silent, but commonly so far apart bodily that we cannot possibly hear each other's voice in any case. Referred to this standard, speech is for the convenience of those who are hard of hearing; but there are many fine things which we cannot say if we have to shout. As the conversation began to assume a loftier and grander tone, we gradually shoved our chairs far-ther apart till they touched the wall in opposite corners, and then commonly there was not enough room.

Walden, "Visitors"

The Dinners You Give

If any ever went away disappointed or hungry from my
house when they found me at home, they may depend
upon it that I sympathized with them at least. So easy is
it, though many housekeepers doubt it, to establish new
and better customs in the place of old. You need not
rest your reputation on the dinners you give. For my
own part, I was never so effectually deterred from fre-
quenting a man's house, by any kind of Cerberus[20]
whatever, as by the parade one made about dining me,
which I took to be a very polite and round-about hint
never to trouble him again.

Walden, "Visitors"

On Cape Cod, Part 3:
Poor Good-for-Nothing Critturs

Houses near the sea are generally low and broad. These
were a story and a half high; but if you merely counted
the windows in their gable-ends, you would think that
there were many stories more, or, at any rate, that the
half-story was the only one thought worthy of being
illustrated. The great number of windows in the ends of
the houses, and their irregularity in size and position,
here and elsewhere on the Cape, struck us agreeably, —
as if each of the various occupants who had their *cuna-
bula* behind had punched a hole where his necessities
required it, and, according to his size and stature,

---

[20] Cerberus: from Greek mythology, a three-headed dog that
guards the entrance to the underworld

without regard to outside effect. There were windows for the grown folks and windows for the children, — three or four apiece; as a certain man had a large hole cut in his barn-door for the cat, and another smaller one for the kitten. Sometimes they were so low under the eaves that I thought they must have perforated the plate beam for another apartment, and I noticed some which were triangular, to fit that part more exactly. The ends of the houses had thus as many muzzles as a revolver, and, if the inhabitants have the same habit of staring out the windows that some of our neighbors have, a traveller must stand a small chance with them.

Generally, the old-fashioned and unpainted houses on the Cape looked more comfortable, as well as picturesque, than the modern and more pretending ones, which were less in harmony with the scenery, and less firmly planted.

These houses were on the shores of a chain of ponds, seven in number, the source of a small stream called Herring River, which empties into the Bay. There are many Herring Rivers on the Cape; they will, perhaps, be more numerous than herrings soon. We knocked at the door of the first house, but its inhabitants were all gone away. In the meanwhile, we saw the occupants of the next one looking out the window at us, and before we reached it an old woman came out and fastened the door of her bulkhead, and went in again. Nevertheless, we did not hesitate to knock at her door, when a grizzly-looking man appeared, whom we took to be sixty or seventy years old. He asked us, at first suspiciously, where we were from, and what our business was; to which we returned plain answers.

"How far is Concord from Boston?" he inquired.

"Twenty miles by railroad."

"Twenty miles by railroad," he repeated.

"Didn't you ever hear of Concord of Revolutionary fame?"

"Didn't I ever hear of Concord? Why, I heard the guns fire at the battle of Bunker Hill. [They hear the sound of heavy cannon across the Bay.] I am almost ninety; I am eighty-eight year old. I was fourteen year old at the time of Concord Fight, — and where were you then?"

We were obliged to confess that we were not in the fight.

"Well, walk in, we'll leave it to the women," said he.

So we walked in, surprised, and sat down, an old woman taking our hats and bundles, and the old man continued, drawing up to the large, old-fashioned fireplace, —

"I am a poor good-for-nothing crittur, as Isaiah says; I am all broken down this year. I am under petticoat government here."

The family consisted of the old man, his wife, and his daughter, who appeared nearly as old as her mother, a fool, her son (a brutish-looking, middle-aged man, with a prominent lower face, who was standing by the hearth when we entered, but immediately went out), and a little boy of ten.

While my companion talked with the women, I

talked with the old man. They said that he was old and foolish, but he was evidently too knowing for them.

"These women," said he to me, "are both of them poor good-for-nothing critturs. This one is my wife. I married her sixty-four years ago. She is eighty-four years old and as deaf as an adder, and the other is not much better."

He thought well of the Bible, or at least he *spoke* well and did not *think* ill of it, for that would not have been prudent for a man of his age. He said that he had read it attentively for many years, and he had much of it at his tongue's end. He seemed deeply impressed with a sense of his own nothingness and would repeatedly exclaim, "I am a nothing. What I gather from my Bible is just this: that man is a poor good-for-nothing crittur, and everything is just as God sees fit and disposes."

"May I ask your name?" I said.

"Yes," he answered, "I am not ashamed to tell my name. My name is ——. My great-grandfather came over from England and settled here."

He was an old Wellfleet oysterman, who had acquired a competency in that business, and had sons still engaged in it. …

Cape Cod

Weighing In

When I read the other day the weight of some of the generals of the Revolution, it seemed no unimportant fact in their biography — It is at least one other means of comparing ourselves with them — Tell me how much Milton or Shakespeare weighed and I will get weighed myself, that I may know better what they are to me.

Weight has something very imposing in it — for we cannot get rid of it. Once in the scales we must weigh — And are we not always in the scales, and weighing just our due, though we kick the beam, and do all we can to heavy or lighten ourselves?

Journal: February 2, 1841

Waldo's Gun

Emerson is gone to the Adirondack country with a hunting party. Eddy says he has carried a double-barrelled gun, one side for shot, the other for ball, for Lowell[21] killed a bear there last year. But the story on

---

[21] James Russell Lowell, first editor of *The Atlantic Monthly* and author of *A Fable for Critics* (1847), a bit of doggerel that ridiculed Thoreau as an Emersonian poseur (Thoreau himself was aware of the piece). Earlier the same year, Lowell solicited an article from Thoreau for *The Atlantic.* When the article, about the Maine woods, was published, Thoreau discovered that Lowell had cut a sentence without his approval. On June 22, 1858, Thoreau wrote Lowell in outrage: "I hardly need to say that this is a liberty which I will not permit to be taken with my MS. The editor has, in this case, no more right to omit a sentiment than to insert one, or put words into my mouth. I feel this treatment to be an insult. ... I am not willing to be associated in any way, unnecessarily, with parties who will confess themselves so bigoted & timid as this implies. ... Is this the avowed character of the Atlantic Monthly? I should like an early reply." It is unknown whether Lowell ever answered. On October 4, 1858, Thoreau wrote again, complaining that despite earlier requests, he had not yet been paid for the article. "Your magazine is indebted to me for thirty-three pages at six dollars a page—$198." Thoreau refused to write again for *The Atlantic*

the Mill-Dam is that he has taken a gun which throws shot from one end and ball from the other!

Journal: August 6, 1858

Waldo's Gun, Again

Emerson says that he and Agassiz and Company broke some dozens of ale-bottles, one after another, with their bullets, in the Adirondack Country, using them for marks! It sounds rather Cockneyish. He says that he shot a peetweet for Agassiz, and this, I think he said, was the first game he ever bagged. He carried a double-barrelled gun, — rifle and shotgun, — which he bought for the purpose, which he says received much commendation, — all parties thought it a very pretty piece. Think of Emerson shooting a peetweet (with shot) for Agassiz, and cracking an ale-bottle (after emptying it) with his rifle at six rods! They cut several pounds of lead out of the tree.

Journal: August 23, 1858

Hosmer's Horn

Hosmer is haying, but inclined to talk as usual. I blowed on his horn at supper-time. I asked if I should

---

until the editorship changed three years later. In 1865 Lowell would publish in *The North American Review* a mean-spirited posthumous attack on Thoreau and his work. The 1858 hunting excursion included, in addition to Lowell and Emerson, William James Stillman and the naturalist Louis Agassiz, among others. As noted by Thoreau Institute curator Jeffrey S. Cramer, Henry Wadsworth Longfellow was encouraged to join, but upon learning that the hunting party included a gun-toting Emerson, he refused and exclaimed, "Then somebody will be shot!"

do any harm if I sounded it. He said no, but I called Mrs. Hosmer back, who was on her way to the village, though I blowed it but poorly.

Journal: July 6, 1852

Off the Handle

My practicalness is not to be trusted to the last. To be sure, I go upon my legs for the most part, but, being hard-pushed and dogged by a superficial common sense which is bound to near objects by beaten paths, I am off the handle, as the phrase is, — I begin to be transcend-ental and show where my heart is. I am like those guinea fowl which Charles Darwin saw at the Cape de Verd Islands. He says, "They avoided us like partridges on a rainy day in September, running with their heads cocked up; and if pursued, they readily took to the wing."

It is a certain faeryland where we live. I wonder that I ever get five miles on my way, the walk is so crowded with events and phenomena. How many questions there are which I have not put to the inhabitants!

But how far can you carry *your* practicalness? How far does your knowledge really extend? When I have read in deeds only a hundred years old the words "to enjoy and possess, he and his assigns, *forever*," I have seen how short-sighted is the sense which conducts from day to day. When I read the epitaphs of those who died a century ago, they seem deader even than they expected. A day seems proportionally a long part of your "forever and a day."

Journal: June 7, 1850

My Fungus

Saturday. 4 A.M. By boat to Nawshawtuct; to Azalea Spring, or Pinxter Spring.

As I was going up the hill, I was surprised to see rising above the June-grass, near a walnut, a whitish object, like a stone with a white top, or a skunk erect, for it was black below. It was an enormous toadstool, or fungus, a sharply conical parasol in the form of a sugar loaf, slightly turned up at the edges, which were rent half an inch in every inch or two. The whole height was sixteen inches. The pileus or cap was six inches long by seven in width at the rim, though it appeared longer than wide. There was no veil, and the stem was about one inch in diameter and naked.

It looked much like an old felt hat that is pushed up into a cone and its rim all ragged and with some meal shaken onto it; in fact, it was almost big enough for a child's head. It was so delicate and fragile that its whole cap trembled on the least touch, and, as I could not lay it down without injuring it, I was obliged to carry it home all the way in my hand and erect, while I paddled my boat with one hand. It was a wonder how its soft cone ever broke through the earth. Such growths ally our age to former periods, such as geology reveals. I wondered if it had not some relation to the skunk, though not in odor, yet in its colors and the general impression it made. It suggests a vegetative force which may almost make man tremble for his dominion. It carries me back to the era of the formation of the coal-measures — the age of the saurus and pleiosaurus and when bullfrogs were as big as bulls. Its stem had something massy about it like an oak, large in proportion to the weight it had to support (though not perhaps to the size of the cap), like the vast hollow columns under some piazzas, whose caps have hardly weight enough to hold their tops together. It made you think of parasols of Chinese mandarins; or it might have been used by the great fossil bullfrog in his walks. What part does it play in the economy of the world?

I have just been out (7.30 A.M.) to show my fungus. The milkman and the butcher followed me to inquire what it was, and children and young ladies addressed me in the street who never spoke to me before. It was so fragile I was obliged to walk at a funereal pace for fear of jarring it. It is so delicately balanced on its stem that it falls to one side across it on the least inclination; falls about like an umbrella that has lost its stays. It is rapidly curling up on the edge, and the rents increasing, until it is completely fringed, and is an inch wider there. It is melting in the sun and light, and black drops and streams falling on my hand and fragments of the black fringed rim falling on the sidewalk. Evidently such a plant can only be seen in perfection in the early morning. It is a creature of the night, like the great moths. They wish me to send it to the first of a series of exhibitions of flowers and fruits to be held at the court-house this afternoon, which I promise to do if it is presentable then. Perhaps it might be placed in the court-house cellar and the company be invited at last to walk down and examine it. Think of placing this giant parasol fungus in the midst of all their roses; yet they admit that it would overshadow and eclipse them all. It is to be remarked that this grew, not in low and damp soil, but high up on the open side of a dry hill, about two rods from a walnut and one from a wall, in the midst of and rising above the thin June-grass. The last night was warm; the earth was very dry, and there was a slight sprinkling of rain. …

I put the parasol fungus in the cellar to preserve it, but it went on rapidly melting and wasting away from the edges upward, spreading as it dissolved, till it was shaped like a dish cover. By night, though kept in the cellar all the day, there was not more than two of the six inches of the height of the cap left, and the barrel-head beneath it and its own stem looked as if a large bottle of ink had been broken there. It defiled all it touched. Probably one night produced it, and in one day, with all our pains, it wasted away. Is it not a giant mildew or mould? The Pyramids and other monuments of Egypt are a vast mildew or toadstools which have met with no light of day sufficient to waste them away. Slavery is such a mould, and superstition, — which are most rank in the warm and humid portions of the globe. Luxor sprang up one night out of the slime of the Nile. The humblest, puniest weed that can endure the sun is thus superior to the largest fungus, as is the peasant's cabin to those foul temples. It is a temple consecrated to

Apis.[22] All things flower, both vices and virtues, but the one is essentially foul, the other fair. In hell, toadstools should be represented as overshadowing men.

Journal: June 18, 1853

Or Scrotum

Found amid the sphagnum on the dry bank on the south side of the Turnpike, just below Everett's meadow, a rare and remarkable fungus, such as I have heard of but never seen before. The whole height six and three quarter inches, two thirds of it being buried in the sphagnum. It may be divided into three parts, pileus, stem, and base, — or scrotum, for it is a perfect phallus. One of those fungi named *impudicus*, I think. In all respects a most disgusting object, yet very suggestive. It is hollow from top to bottom, the form of the hollow answering to that of the outside. The color of the outside white excepting the pileus, which is olive-colored and somewhat coarsely corrugated, with an oblong mouth at tip about one eighth of an inch long, or, measuring the white lips, half an inch. ... It is a delicate white cylinder of a finely honeycombed and crispy material about three sixteenths of an inch thick, or more, the whole very straight and regular. The base, or scrotum, is of an irregular bag form, about one inch by two in the extremes, consisting of a thick trembling gelatinous mass surrounding the bottom of the stem and covered with a tough white skin of a darker tint

---

[22] Apis: the genus of the honeybee

than the stem. The whole plant rather frail and trembling. There was at first a very thin delicate white collar (or *volva?*) about the base of the stem above the scrotum. It was as offensive to the eye as to the scent, the cap rapidly melting and defiling what it touched with a fetid, olivaceous, semiliquid matter. In an hour or two the plant scented the whole

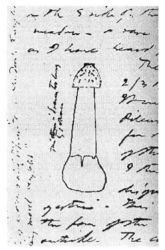

Drawing by Thoreau

house wherever placed, so that it could not be endured. I was afraid to sleep in my chamber where it had lain until the room had been well ventilated. It smelled like a dead rat in the ceiling, in all the ceilings of the house. Pray, what was Nature thinking when she made this? She almost puts herself on a level with those who draw in privies.

Journal: October 16, 1856

Humors or Pimples

In the low woodland paths full of rank weeds, there are countless great fungi of various forms and colors, the produce of the warm rains and muggy weather of a week ago, now rapidly dissolving. One great one, more than a foot in diameter, with a stem 2½+ inches through and 5 inches high, and which has sprung up since I passed here on the 10th, is already sinking like lead into that portion already melted. The ground is covered with foul spots where they have dissolved, and for *most* of my *walk* the air is tainted with a musty, carrion-like odor, in some places very offensive, so that I at first suspected a dead horse or cow. They impress me like humors or pimples on the face of the earth, toddy-blossoms, by which it gets rid of its corrupt blood. A sort of excrement they are.

Journal: August 14, 1853

Statues

Dr. Bartlett handed me a paper today, desiring me to subscribe to a statue for Horace Mann. I declined and said that I thought a man ought not anymore to take up room in the world after he was dead. We shall lose our advantage of a man's dying if we are to have a statue of him forthwith. This is probably meant to be an opposition statue to that of Webster. At this rate they will crowd the streets with them. A man will have to add a clause to his will, "No statue to be made of me." It is very offensive to my imagination to see the dying stiffen into statues at this rate. We should wait till their bones begin to crumble — and then avoid too near a likeness to the living.

Journal: September 18, 1859

Man the Eel, or: Hope of Rudeness

Men are very generally spoiled by being so civil and well-disposed. You can have no profitable conversation with them, they are so conciliatory, determined to agree with you. They exhibit such long-suffering and kind-ness in a short interview. I would meet with some provoking strangeness, so that we may be guest and host and refresh one another. It is possible for a man wholly to disappear and be merged in his manners. The thousand and one gentlemen whom I meet, I meet despairingly, and but to part from them, for I am not cheered by the hope of any rudeness from them. A cross man, a coarse man, an eccentric man, a silent, a man who does not drill well, — of him there is some hope. Your gentlemen, they are all alike. They utter their opinions as if it was not a man that uttered them. It is "just as you please;" they are indifferent to everything. They will talk with you for nothing. The interesting man will rather avoid [you], and it is a rare chance if you get so far as talk with him. The laborers whom I know, the loafers, fishers, and hunters, I can spin yarns with profitably, for it is hands off; they are they and I am I still; they do not come to me and quarter them-selves on me for a day or an hour to be treated politely, they do not approach me with a flag of truce. They do not go out of themselves to meet me. I am never electri-fied by my gentleman; he is not an electric eel but one of the common kind that slip through your hands, how-ever hard you clutch them, and leave them covered with slime.

Journal: July 21, 1851

To Have & Possess

How, when a man purchases a thing, he is determined
to get and get hold of it, using how many expletives
and how long a string of synonymous or similar terms
signifying possession, in the legal process! What's
mine's my own. An old deed of a small piece of swamp
land, which I have lately surveyed at the risk of being
mired past recovery, says that "the said Spaulding his
Heirs and Assigns, shall and may from this time, and at
all times forever hereafter, by force and virtue of these
presents, lawfully, peacably and quietly have, hold, use,
occupy, possess and enjoy the said swamp," etc.

Journal: February 12, 1850

Dividing Stock

When two men, Billings and Prichard, were dividing
the stock of my father and Hurd, the former acting for
Father, P. was rather tight for Hurd. They came to a
cracked bowl, at which P. hesitated and asked, "Well,
what shall we do with this?" B. took it in haste and
broke it, and, presenting him one piece, said, "There,
that is your half and this is ours."

Journal: December 31, 1855

Ambitious Booby

Nations are possessed with an insane ambition to per-
petuate the memory of themselves by the amount of
hammered stone they leave. What if equal pains were
taken to smooth and polish their manners? One piece of
good sense would be more memorable than a monu-

ment as high as the moon. I love better to see stones in place. The grandeur of Thebes was a vulgar grandeur. More sensible is a rod of stone wall that bounds an honest man's field than a hundred-gated Thebes that has wandered farther from the true end of life. The religion and civilization which are barbaric and heathenish build splendid temples; but what you might call Christianity does not. Most of the stone a nation hammers goes toward its tomb only. It buries itself alive. As for the Pyramids, there is nothing to wonder at in them so much as the fact that so many men could be found degraded enough to spend their lives constructing a tomb for some ambitious booby, whom it would have been wiser and manlier to have drowned in the Nile, and then given his body to the dogs. I might possibly invent some excuse for them and him, but I have no time for it. As for the religion and love of art of the builders, it is much the same all the world over, whether the building be an Egyptian temple or the United States Bank. It costs more than it comes to. ... As for your high towers and monuments, there was a crazy fellow once in this town who undertook to dig through to China, and he got so far that, as he said, he heard the Chinese pots and kettles rattle; but I think that I shall not go out of my way to admire the hole which he made. Many are concerned about the monuments of the West and the East, — to know who built them. For my part, I should like to know who in those days did not build them, — who were above such trifling.

Walden, "Economy"

Owl Adoption

As I paddle under the Hemlock bank this cloudy afternoon, about 3 o'clock, I see a screech owl sitting on the edge of a hollow hemlock stump about three feet high, at the base of a large hemlock. It sits with its head drawn in, eyeing me, with its eyes partly open, about twenty feet off. When it hears me move, it turns its head toward me, perhaps one eye only open, with its great glaring golden iris. You see two whitish triangular lines above the eyes meeting at the bill, with a sharp reddish-brown triangle between and a narrow curved line of black under each eye. At this distance and in this light, you see only a black spot where the eye is, and the question is whether the eyes are open or not. It sits on the lee side of the tree this raw and windy day. You would say that this was a bird without a neck. Its short bill, which rests upon its breast, scarcely projects at all, but in a state of rest the whole upper part of the bird from the wings is rounded off smoothly, excepting the horns, which stand up conspicuously or are slanted back. After watching it ten minutes from the boat, I landed two rods above, and, stealing quietly up behind the hemlock, though from the windward, I looked carefully around it, and, to my surprise, saw the owl still sitting there. So I sprang round quickly, with my arm outstretched, and caught it in my hand. It was so surprised that it offered no resistance at first, only glared at me in mute astonishment with eyes as big as saucers. But ere long it began to snap its bill, making quite a noise, and, as I rolled it up in my handkerchief and put it in my pocket, it bit my finger slightly. I soon took it out of my pocket and, tying the handkerchief, left it on the bottom of the boat. So I carried it home and made a small cage in which to keep it, for a night. When I took it up, it clung so tightly to my hand as to sink its claws into my fingers and bring blood.

When alarmed or provoked most, it snaps its bill and hisses. It puffs up its feathers to nearly twice its usual size, stretches out its neck, and, with wide-open eyes, stares this way and that, moving its head slowly and undulatingly from side to side with a curious motion. While I write this evening, I see that there is ground for much superstition in it. It looks out on me from a dusky corner of its box with its great solemn eyes, so perfectly still itself. I was surprised to find that I could imitate its note as I remember it, by a *guttural* whinnering.

A remarkably squat figure, being very broad in proportion to its length, with a short tail, and very catlike in the face with its horns and great eyes. Remarkably large feet and talons, legs thickly clothed with whitish down, down to the talons. It brought blood from my fingers by clinging to them. It would lower its head, stretch out its neck, and, bending it from side to side, peer at you with laughable circumspection; from side to side, as if to catch or absorb into its eyes every ray of light, strain at you with complacent yet earnest scrutiny. Raising and lowering its head and moving it from side to side in a slow and regular manner, at the same time snapping its bill smartly perhaps, and faintly hissing, and puffing itself up more and more, — cat-like, turtle-like, both in hissing and swelling. The slowness and gravity, not to say solemnity, of this motion are striking. There plainly is no jesting in this case.

General color of the owl a rather pale and perhaps slightly reddish brown, the feathers centred with black. Perches with two claws above and two below the perch. It is a slight body, covered with a mass of soft and light-lying feathers. Its head muffled in a great hood. It must be quite comfortable in winter. Dropped a pellet of fur and bones in his cage. He sat, not really moping but trying to sleep, in a corner of his box all day, yet with one or both eyes slightly open all the while. I never once caught him with his eyes shut. Ordinarily stood rather than sat on his perch.

Journal: October 28, 1855

Owl Astonishment

P.M.—Up Assabet.

Carried my owl to the hill again. Had to shake him out of the box, for he did not go of his own accord. (He had learned to alight on his perch, and it was surprising how lightly and noiselessly he would hop upon it.) There he stood on the grass, at first bewildered, with his horns pricked up and looking toward me. In this strong light the pupils of his eyes suddenly contracted and the iris expanded till they were two great orbs with a centre spot merely. His attitude expressed astonishment more than anything. I was obliged to toss him up a little that he might feel his wings, and then he flapped away low and heavy to a hickory on the hillside twenty rods off. (I had let him out in the plain just east of the hill.) Thither I followed and tried to start him again. As I moved around him, he turned his head always toward me, till he looked *directly* behind himself as he sat crosswise on a bough. He behaved as if bewildered and dazzled, gathering all the light he could and ever straining his great eyes toward you to make out who you are, but not inclining to fly. He never appeared so much alarmed as surprised and astonished.

Journal: October 29, 1855

You Might Get Into the Papers

I have several friends and acquaintances who are very good companions in the house or for an afternoon walk, but whom I cannot make up my mind to make a longer excursion with; for I discover, all at once, that they are too gentlemanly in manners, dress, and all their habits. I see in my mind's eye that they wear black coats, considerable starched linen, glossy hats and shoes, and it is out of the question. It is a great disadvantage for a traveller to be a gentleman of this kind; he is so ill-treated, only a prey to landlords. It would be too much of a circumstance to enter a strange town or house with such a companion. You could not travel incognito; you might get into the papers. You should travel as a common man. If such a one were to set out to make a walking-journey, he would betray himself at every step. Everyone would see that he was trying an experiment, as plainly as they see that a lame man is lame by his limping. The natives would bow to him, other gentlemen would invite him to ride, conductors would warn him that this was the second-class car, and many would take him for a clergyman; and so he would be continually pressed and balked and run upon. You would not see the natives at all. Instead of going in quietly at the back door and sitting by the kitchen fire, you would be shown into a cold parlor, there to confront a fireboard, and excite a commotion in a whole family. The women would scatter at your approach, and their husbands and sons would go right up to hunt up their black coats, — for they all have them; they are as cheap as dirt. You would go trailing your limbs along the highways, mere bait for corpulent innholders, as a pickerel's leg[23] is trolled along a stream, and your part of the profits would be the frog's. No, you must be a common man, or at least travel as one, and then nobody will know that you are there or have been there. I will not undertake a simple pedestrian excursion with one of these, because to enter a village, or a hotel, with such a one, would be too great a circumstance, would create too great a stir. You could only go half as far with the same means, for the price of board and lodgings would rise everywhere;

---

[23] A frog leg, often used as bait while fishing for pickerel

so much you have to pay for wearing that kind of coat.

Journal: June 3, 1857

Untied

I have for years had a great deal of trouble with my shoe-strings, because they get untied continually. They are leather, rolled and tied in a hard knot. But some days I could hardly go twenty rods before I was obliged to stop and stoop to tie my shoes. My companion and I speculated on the distance to which one tying would carry you, — the length of a shoe-tie, — and we thought it nearly as appreciable and certainly a more simple and natural measure of distance than a stadium, or league, or mile. Ever and anon we raised our feet on to whatever fence or wall or rock or stump we chanced to be passing, and drew the strings once more, pulling as hard as we could. It was very vexacious, when passing through low scrubby bushes, to become conscious that the strings were already getting loose again before we had fairly started. What should we have done if pursued by a tribe of Indians? My companion sometimes went without strings altogether, but that loose way of proceeding was not to be thought of by me. One shoemaker sold us shoe-strings made of the hide of a South American jackass, which he recommended; or rather he gave them to us and added their price to that of the shoes we bought of him. But I could not see that these were any better than the old. I wondered if anybody had exhibited a better article at the World's Fair, and whether England did not bear the palm from

America in this respect. I thought of strings with recurved prickles and various other remedies myself. At last the other day it occurred to me that I would try an experiment, and, instead of tying two simple knots one over the other the same way, putting the end which fell to the right over each time, that I would reverse the process, and put it under the other. Greatly to my satisfaction, the experiment was perfectly successful, and from that time my shoe-strings have given me no trouble, except sometimes in untying them at night.

Journal: July 25, 1843

The Boot Salesman's Rigmarole

When I bought my boots yesterday, Hastings ran over his usual rigmarole. Had he any stout old-fashioned cowhide boots? Yes, he thought he could suit me. "There's something that 'll turn water about as well as anything. Billings had a pair just like them the other day, and he said they kept his feet as dry as a bone. But what's more than that, they were made above a year ago upon honor. They are just the thing, you may depend on it. I had an eye to you when I was making them." "But they are too soft and thin for me. I want them to be thick and stand out from my foot." "Well, there is another pair, maybe a little thicker. I'll tell you what it is, these are made of dry hide."

Both were warranted single leather and not split. I took the last. But after wearing them round this cold day I found that the little snow which rested on them and melted wet the upper leather through like paper and wet my feet, and I told H. of it, that he might have an offset to Billings's experience. "Well, you can't expect a new pair of boots to turn water at first. I tell the farmers that the time to buy boots is at midsummer, or when they are hoeing their potatoes, and the pores have a chance to get filled with dirt."

Journal: December 4, 1856

The Moodiest Person, or:
The Frame to My Pictures

In our walks C.[24] takes out his notebook sometimes and tries to write as I do, but all in vain. He soon puts it up again, or contents himself with scrawling some sketch of the landscape. Observing me still scribbling, he will say that he confines himself to the ideal, purely ideal remarks; he leaves the facts to me. Sometimes, too, he will say a little petulantly, "*I* am universal; I have nothing to do with the particular and definite." He is the moodiest person, perhaps, that I ever saw. As naturally whimsical as a cow is brindled, both in his tenderness and his roughness he belies himself. He can be incredibly selfish and unexpectedly generous. He is conceited, and yet there is in him far more than usual to ground conceit upon.

I, too, would fain set down something beside facts. Facts should only be as the frame to my pictures; they should be material to the mythology which I am writing; not facts to assist men to make money, farmers to

---

[24] William Ellery Channing. See also note, page 61.

farm profitably, in any common sense; facts to tell who I am, and where I have been or what I have thought: as now the bell rings for evening meeting, and its volumes of sound, like smoke which rises from where a cannon is fired, make the tent in which I dwell. I would so state facts that they shall be significant, shall be myths or mythologic. Facts which the mind perceived, thoughts which the body thought.

Journal: November 9, 1851

Sunbeams

I must confess I have felt mean enough when asked how I was to act on society, what errand I had to mankind. Undoubtedly I did not feel mean without a reason, and yet my loitering is not without defense. I would fain communicate the wealth of my life to men, would really give them what is most precious in my gift. I would secrete pearls with the shellfish and lay up honey with the bees for them. I will sift the sunbeams for the public good. I know no riches I would keep back. I have no private good, unless it be my peculiar ability to serve the public. This is the only individual property. Each one may thus be innocently rich. I inclose and foster the pearl till it is grown. I wish to communicate those parts of my life which I would gladly live again myself.

Journal: March 26, 1842

On Cape Cod, Part 4:
It Would Kill a Cat

Our host told us that the sea-clam, or hen, was not easily obtained; it was raked up, but never on the Atlantic side, only cast ashore there in small quantities in storms. The fisherman sometimes wades in water several feet deep, and thrusts a pointed stick into the sand before him. When this enters between the valves of a clam, he closes them on it, and is drawn out. It has been known to catch and hold coot and teal which were preying on it. I chanced to be on the bank of the Acushnet at New Bedford one day since this, watching some ducks, when a man informed me that, having let out his young ducks to seek their food amid the samphire (*Salicornia*) and other weeds along the riverside at low tide that morning, at length he noticed that one remained stationary amid the weeds, something preventing it from following the others, and going to it he found its foot tightly shut in a quahog's[25] shell. He took up both together, carried them to his home, and his wife opening the shell with a knife released the duck and cooked the quahog. The old man said that the great clams were good to eat, but that they always took out a certain part which was poisonous before they cooked them. "People said it would kill a cat." I did not tell him that I had eaten a large one entire that afternoon, but I began to think that I was tougher than a cat. …

---

[25] Quahog (sometimes quahaug): common name for the hard clam

At length the fool, whom my companion called the wizard, came in, muttering between his teeth, "Damn book-pedlers, — all the time talking about books. Better do something. Damn 'em. I'll shoot 'em. Got a doctor down here. Damn him, I'll get a gun and shoot him"; never once holding up his head. Whereat the old man stood up and said in a loud voice, as if he was accustomed to command, and this was not the first time he had been obliged to exert his authority there: "John, go sit down, mind your business, — we've heard you talk before, — precious little you'll do, — your bark is worse than your bite." But, without minding, John muttered the same gibberish over again, and then sat down at the table which the old folks had left. He ate all there was on it, and then turned to the apples, which his aged mother was paring, that she might give her guests some applesauce for breakfast, but she drew them away and sent him off. ...

This was the merriest old man that we had ever seen, and one of the best preserved. His style of conversation was coarse and plain enough to have suited Rabelais. ... There was a strange mingling of past and present in his conversation, for he had lived under King George, and might have remembered when Napolean and the moderns generally were born. ... He remembered well George Washington and how he rode his horse along the streets of Boston, and he stood up to show us how he looked.

"He was a r—a—ther large and portly-looking man, a manly and resolute-looking officer, with a pretty good leg as he sat on his horse." — "There, I'll tell you, this was the way with Washington." Then he jumped up again, and bowed gracefully to right and left, making show as if he were waving his hat. Said he, "*That* was Washington."

He told us many anecdotes of the Revolution, and was much pleased when we told him that we had read the same in history and that his account agreed with the written.

"O," he said, "I know, I know! I was a young fellow of sixteen, with my ears wide open; and a fellow of that age, you know, is pretty wide awake, and likes to know everything that's going on. O, I know!"…

In the course of the evening I began to feel the potency of the clam which I had eaten, and I was obliged to confess to our host that I was no tougher than the cat he told of; but he answered that he was a plainspoken man and he could tell me that it was all imagination. At any rate, it proved an emetic in my case, and I was made quite sick by it for a short time, while he laughed at my expense. I was pleased to read afterward, in Mourt's Relation of the landing of the Pilgrims in Provincetown Harbor, these words: "We found great muscles (the old editor says that they were undoubtedly sea-clams) and very fat and full of sea pearl; but we could not eat them for they made us all sick that did eat, as well sailors as passengers, … but they were soon well again." It brought me nearer to the Pilgrims to be thus reminded by a similar experience that I was so like them. Moreover, it was an invaluable confirmation of their story, and I am prepared now to believe every word of Mourt's Relation. I was also pleased to find that man and the clam lay still at the same angle to one another. But I did not notice sea-pearl. Like Cleopatra, I must have swallowed it. ...

Cape Cod

Accidental Arson

I once set fire to the woods. Having set out, one April day, to go to the sources of the Concord River in a boat with a single companion, meaning to camp on the bank at night or seek a lodging in some neighboring country inn or farmhouse, we took fishing tackle with us that we might fitly procure our food from the stream, Indian-like. At the shoemaker's near the river, we obtained a match, which we had forgotten. Though it was thus early in the spring, the river was low, for there had not been much rain, and we succeeded in catching a mess of fish sufficient for our dinner before we had left the town, and by the shore of Fair Haven Pond we proceeded to cook them. The earth was uncommonly dry, and our fire, kindled far from the woods in a sunny recess in the hillside on the east of the pond, suddenly caught the dry grass of the previous year which grew about the stump on which it was kindled. We sprang to extinguish it at first with our hands and feet, and then we fought it with a board obtained from the boat, but in a few minutes it was beyond our reach; being on the side of a hill, it spread rapidly upward, through the long, dry, wiry grass interspersed with bushes.

"Well, where will this end?" asked my companion. I saw that it might be bounded by Well Meadow Brook on one side, but would, perchance, go to the village side of the brook. "It will go to town," I answered. While my companion took the boat back down the river, I set out through the woods to inform the owners and to raise the town. The fire had already spread a dozen rods on every side and went leaping and crackling wildly and irreclaimably toward the wood. That way went the flames with wild delight, and we felt that we had no control over the demonic creature to which we had given birth. We had kindled many fires in the woods before, burning a clear space in the grass, without ever kindling such a fire as this.

As I ran toward the town through the woods, I could see the smoke over the woods behind me marking the spot and the progress of the flames. The first farmer whom I met driving a team, after leaving the woods, inquired the cause of the smoke. I told him. "Well," said he, "it is none of my stuff," and drove along. The next I met was the owner in his field, with whom I returned at once to the woods, running all the way. I had already run two miles. When at length we got into the neighborhood of the flames, we met a carpenter who had been hewing timber, an infirm man who had been driven off by the fire, fleeing with his axe. The farmer returned to hasten more assistance. I, who was spent with running, remained. What could I do alone against a front of flame half a mile wide?

I walked slowly through the wood to Fair Haven Cliff, climbed to the highest rock, and sat down upon it to observe the progress of the flames, which were rapidly approaching me, now about a mile distant from the spot where the fire was kindled. Presently I heard the sound of the distant bell giving the alarm, and I knew that the town was on its way to the scene. Hitherto I had felt like a guilty person, — nothing but shame and regret. But now I settled the matter with myself shortly. I said to myself: "Who are these men who are said to be the owners of these woods, and how am I related to them? I have set fire to the forest, but I have done no wrong therein, and now it is as if the lightning had done it. These flames are but consuming their natural food." (It has never troubled me from that day to this more than if the lightning had done it. The trivial fishing was all that disturbed me and disturbs me still.) So shortly I settled it with myself and stood to watch the approaching flames. It was a glorious spectacle, and I was the only one there to enjoy it. The fire now reached the base of the cliff and then rushed up its sides. The squirrels ran before it in blind haste, and three pigeons dashed into the midst of the smoke. The flames flashed up the pines to their tops, as if they were powder.

When I found I was about to be surrounded by the fire, I retreated and joined the forces now arriving from the town. It took us several hours to surround the flames with our hoes and shovel and by back fires subdue them. In the midst of all I saw the farmer whom I first met, who had turned indifferently away saying it was none of his stuff, striving earnestly to save his corded wood, which the fire had already seized and which it after all consumed.

It burned over a hundred acres or more and destroyed much young wood. When I returned home late in the day, with others of my townsmen, I could not help noticing that the crowd who were so ready to condemn the individual who had kindled the fire did not sympathize with the owners of the wood, but were in fact highly elate and as it were thankful for the opportunity which had afforded them so much sport; and it was only half a dozen owners, so called, though not all of them, who looked sour or grieved, and I felt that I had a deeper interest in the woods, knew them better and should feel their loss more, than any or all of them. The farmer whom I had first conducted to the woods was obliged to ask me the shortest way back, through his own lot. Why, then, should the half dozen owners [and] the individuals who set the fire alone feel sorrow for the loss of the wood, while the rest of the town have their spirits raised? Some of the owners, however, bore their loss like men, but other some declared behind my back that I was a "damned rascal;" and a flibbertigibbet or two, who crowed like the old cock, shouted some reminiscences of "burnt woods" from safe recesses for some years after. I have nothing to say to any of them. The locomotive engine has since burned over nearly all the same ground and more, and in some measure blotted out the memory of the previous fire. For a long time after I had learned this lesson I marveled that while matches and tinder were contemporaries the world was not consumed; why the houses that have hearths were not burned before another day; if the flames were not as hungry now as when I waked them. I at once ceased to regard the owners and my own fault, — if fault there was any in the matter, — and attended to the phenomenon before me, determined to make the most of it. To be sure, I felt a little ashamed when I reflected on what a trivial occasion this had happened, that at the time I was no better employed than my townsmen.

That night I watched the fire, where some stumps still flamed at midnight in the midst of the blackened waste, wandering through the woods by myself; and far in the night I threaded my way to the spot where the fire had taken, and discovered the now broiled fish, — which had been dressed, — scattered over the burnt grass...[26]

Journal: Undated, 1850

The News

A week or so ago, as I learn, Miss Emeline Barnett told a little boy who boards with her, and who was playing with an open knife in his hand, that he must be careful not to fall down and cut himself with it, for once Mr. David Loring, when he was a little boy, fell down with

---

[26] The fire broke out on April 30, 1844, six years prior to this entry in Thoreau's journal. His companion in setting the fire was Edward Hoar.

a knife in his hand and cut his throat badly. It was soon reported, among the children at least, that little David Loring, the grandson of the former, had fallen down with a knife in his hand as he was going to school, and nearly cut his throat; next, that Mr. David Loring the grandfather (who lives in Framingham) had committed suicide, had cut his throat, was not dead, indeed, but was not expected to live; and in this form the story spread like wildfire over the town and county. Nobody expressed surprise. His oldest acquaintances and best friends, his legal adviser, all said, "Well, I can believe it." He was known by many to have been speculating in Western lands, which, owing to the hard times, was a failure, and he was depressed in consequence. Sally Cummings helped spread the news. Said there was no doubt of it, but there was Fay's wife (L.'s daughter) knew nothing of it yet, they were merry as crickets over there. Others stated that Wetherbee, the expressman, had been over to Northboro, and learned that Mr. Loring had taken poison in Northboro. Mr. Rhodes was stated to have received a letter from Mr. Robbins of Framingham giving all the particulars. Mr. Wild, it was said, had also got a letter from his son Silas in Framingham, to whom he had written, which confirmed the report. As Wild went downtown, he met Meeks the carpenter and inquired in a significant way if he got anything new. Meeks simply answered, "Well, David Loring won't eat another Thanksgiving dinner." A child at school wrote to her parents at Northboro, telling the news. Mrs. Loring's sister lives there, and it chances that her husband committed suicide. They were, therefore, slow to communicate the news to her, but at length could not contain themselves longer and told it. The sister was terribly affected; wrote to her son (L.'s nephew) in Worcester, who immediately took the cars and went to Framingham and when he arrived there met his uncle just putting his family into the cars. He shook his hand very heartily indeed, looking, however, hard at his throat, but said not a word about his errand. Already doubts had arisen, people were careful how they spoke of it, the expressmen were mum, Adams and Wetherbee never said Loring. The Framingham expressman used the same room with Adams in Boston, A. simply asked, "Any news from Framingham this morning? Seen Loring lately?" and learned that all was well.

Journal: November 29, 1857

Run on the Banks

To White Pond. Another, the tenth of these memorable days. We have had some fog the last two or three nights, and this forenoon it was slow to disperse, dog-day-like, but this afternoon it is warmer even than yesterday. I should like it better if it were not so warm. I am glad to reach the shade of Hubbard's Grove; the coolness is refreshing. It is indeed a golden autumn. These ten days are enough to make the reputation of any climate. A tradition of these days might be handed down to posterity. They deserve a notice in history, in the history of Concord. All kinds of crudities have a chance to get ripe this year. Was there ever such an autumn? And yet there was never such a panic and hard times in the commercial world. The merchants and banks are suspending and failing all the country over,[27] but not the sand banks, solid and warm, and streaked with bloody blackberry vines. You may run on them as much as you please, — even as the crickets do, and find their account in it. They are the stockholders in these banks, and I hear then creaking their content. You may see them on change in any warmer hour. In these banks, too, and such as these, are my funds deposited, funds of health and enjoyment. Their (the crickets) prosperity and happiness and, I trust, mine do not depend on whether the New York banks suspend or no. We do not rely on such slender security as the thin paper of the Suffolk Bank. To put your trust in such a bank is to be swallowed up and undergo suffocation. Invest, I say, in these country banks. Let your capital be simplicity and contentment. Withered goldenrod (*Solidago nemoralis*) is no failure, like a broken bank, and yet in its most golden season nobody counterfeits it. I have no compassion for, nor sympathy with, this miserable state of things. Banks built of granite, after some Grecian or Roman style, with their porticoes and their safes of iron, are not so permanent, and cannot give me so good security for capital invested in them, as the heads of withered hardhack in the meadow. I do not

---

[27] Thoreau is referring to the U.S. economic crisis now known as the Panic of 1857.

suspect the solvency of these banks. I know who is their president and cashier.

Journal: October 14, 1857

At an Angle

When some rare northern bird like the pine grosbeak is seen thus far south in the winter, he does not suggest poverty, but dazzles us with his beauty. The woods and fields, now somewhat solitary, being deserted by their more tender summer residents, are now frequented by these rich but delicately tinted and hardy northern immigrants of the air. Here is no imperfection to be suggested. The winter, with its snow and ice, is not an evil to be corrected. It is as it was designed and made to be, for the artist has had leisure to add beauty to use. My acquaintances, angels from the north. I had a vision thus prospectively of these birds as I stood in the swamps. I saw this familiar — too *familiar* fact — at a different angle, and I was charmed and haunted by it. It is only necessary to behold thus the least fact or phenomenon, however familiar, from a point a hair's breadth aside from our habitual path or routine, to be overcome, enchanted by its beauty and significance. Only what we have touched and worn is trivial, — our scurf, repetition, tradition, conformity. To perceive freshly, with fresh senses, is to be inspired. Great winter itself looked like a precious gem, reflecting rainbow colors from one angle.

My body is all sentient. As I go here or there, I am tickled by this or that I come in contact with, as if I

touched the wires of a battery. I can generally recall —
have fresh in my mind — several scratches last received. These I continually recall to mind, reimpress,
and harp upon. The age of miracles is each moment
thus returned. Now it is wild apples, now river reflec-
tions, now a flock of lesser redpolls. In winter, too, re-
sides immortal youth and perennial summer. Its head is
not silvered; its cheek is not blanched but has a ruby
tinge to it.

We get only transient and partial glimpses of the
beauty of the world. Standing at the right angle, we are
dazzled by the colors of the rainbow in colorless ice.
From the right point of view, every storm and every
drop in it is a rainbow. Beauty and music are not mere
traits and exceptions. They are the rule and character.
It is the exception that we see and hear. Then I try to
discover what it was in the vision that charmed and
translated me. What if we could dagguerreotype our
thoughts and feelings! for I am surprised and enchanted
often by some quality which I cannot detect. I have seen
an attribute of another world and condition of things. It
is a wonderful fact that I should be affected, and thus
deeply and powerfully, more than by aught else in my
experience, — that this fruit should be borne in me,
sprung from a seed finer than the spores of fungi, float-
ed from other atmospheres! finer than the dust caught
in the sails of vessels a thousand miles from land! Here
the invisible seeds settle, and spring, and bear flowers
and fruits of immortal beauty.

Journal: December 11, 1855

Dantean Dipper Thieves

One day two young woman — a Sunday — stopped at the door of my hut and asked for some water. I answered that I had no cold water but I would lend them a dipper. They never returned the dipper, and I had a right to suppose that they came to steal. They were a disgrace to their sex and to humanity. Pariahs of the moral world. Evil spirits that thirsted not for water but threw the dipper into the lake. Such as Dante saw. What the lake to them but liquid fire and brimstone? They will never know peace till they have returned the dipper. In all the worlds this is decreed.

Journal: January 17, 1852

How They Do Things in West Acton

As we were walking through West Acton the other afternoon, a few rods only west of the center, on the main road, the Harvard turnpike, we saw a rock larger than a man could lift, lying in the road, exactly in the wheel-track, and were puzzled to tell how it came there, but supposed it had slipped off a drag, — yet we noticed that it was peculiarly black. Returning the same way in the twilight, when we had got within four or five rods of this very spot, looking up, we saw a man in the field, three or four rods on one side of that spot, running off as fast as he could. By the time he had got out of sight over the hill it occurred to us that he was blasting rocks and had just touched one off; so, at the eleventh hour, we turned about and ran the other way, and when we had gone a few rods, off went two blasts, but fortunately none of the rocks struck us. Some time after we had passed we saw the men returning. They looked out for themselves, but for nobody else. This is the way they do things in West Acton. We now understood that the big stone was blackened by powder.

Journal: November 17, 1860

The Stupid

Always you have to contend with the stupidity of men. It is like a stiff soil, a hard-pan. If you go deeper than usual, you are sure to meet with a pan made harder even by the superficial cultivation. The stupid you have always with you. Men are more obedient at first to words than ideas. They mind names more than things. Read to them a lecture on "Education," naming that subject, and they will think that they have heard something important, but call it "Transcendentalism," and they will think it moonshine. Or halve your lecture, and put in a psalm at the beginning and a prayer at the end of it and read it from a pulpit, and they will pronounce it good without thinking.

Journal: February 13, 1860

Titles

When at length, after infinite toil and anxiety, an author has fairly completed his work, the next, and by far the most important concern that demands his attention, is the christening. He is about to send forth his bantling to seek its fortune in the world, and he feels a kind of parental interest in its welfare, prompting him to look about for some expressive and euphonic Title, which, at least, will secure it a civil treatment from mankind, and may, perchance, serve as an introduction to their sincere esteem and regard.

A Title may either be characteristic, consisting of a single expressive word or pithy sentence, or ingenious and amusing, so as to catch the fancy, or excite the curiosity.

… The character of the contents is often quite overlooked in the desire to make a favorable first impression, and the author's whole ingenuity is exerted in the framing of some fanciful or dignified Title, which will at once recommend his book to the favor of the reading public. As some fond parents, in the lower walks of life, are accusomed to ransack the long list of departed worthies for sonorous and well-tried names, or, from the cast-off spoils of the novel heroine, seek to swell the scanty portion which fortune may have allotted to their offspring.

What can be more alluring than the following tempting, and somewhat luxurious display of verbal delicacies — "Paradise of Dainty Devices"? What may be the nature of these "Dainty Devices" is left to be imagined by the reader, it being safer to leave him to his own vague conjectures, than to tell the plain truth at once.

Journal: March 17, 1837

Duds

A wise man will always have his duds picked up, and be ready for whatever may happen — as the prudent merchant, notwithstanding the lavish display of his wares — will yet have them packed or easy to be removed in emergencies. In this sense there is something sluttish in all finery. When I see a fine lady or gentleman dressed to the top of the fashion, I wonder what they would do if an earthquake should happen; or a fire suddenly break out, for they seem to have counted only on fair weather, and that things will go on smoothly and without jostling. Those curls and jewels so nicely adjusted expect an unusual deference from the elements.

Journal: July 12, 1840

Swaggers

The ways by which men express themselves are infinite, — the literary through their writings, and often they do not mind with what air they walk the streets, being sufficiently reported otherwise. But some express themselves chiefly by their gait and carriage, with swelling breasts or elephantine roll and elevated brows, making themselves moving and adequate signs of themselves, having no other outlet. If their greatness had signalized itself sufficiently in some other way, though it were only in picking locks, they could afford to dispense with the swagger.

Journal: August 22, 1852

Bird Flirt

I have often noticed the inquisitiveness of birds, as the other day of a sparrow, whose motions I should not have supposed to have any reference to me, if I had not watched it from first to last. I stood on the edge of a pine and birch wood. It flitted from seven or eight rods distant to a pine within a rod of me, where it hopped about stealthily and chirped awhile, then flew as many rods the other side and hopped about there a spell, then back to the pine again, as near me as it dared, and again to its first position, very restless all the while. Generally I should have supposed that there was more than one bird, or that it was altogether accidental, — that the chipping of this sparrow eight or ten rods away had no reference to me, — for I could see nothing peculiar about it. But when I brought my glass to bear on it, I found that it was almost steadily eyeing me and was all alive with excitement.

Journal: Ooctober 19, 1856

Pig-Headed

3:30 P.M. — When I came forth, thinking to empty my boat and go a-meditating along the river, — for the full ditches and drenched grass forbade other routes, except the highway, — and this is one advantage of a boat, — I learned to my chagrin that Father's pig was gone. He had leaped out of the pen sometime since his breakfast, but his dinner was untouched. Here was an ugly duty not to be shirked, — a wild shoat that weighed but ninety to be tracked, caught, and penned, — an afternoon's work, at least (if I were lucky enough to accomplish it so soon), prepared for me, quite different from what I had anticipated. I felt chagrined, it is true, but I could not ignore the fact nor shirk the duty that lay so near to me. Do the duty that lies nearest to thee. I proposed to Father to sell the pig as he was running (somewhere) to a neighbor who had talked of buying him, making a considerable reduction. But my suggestion was not acted on, and the responsibilities of the case all devolved on me, for I could run faster than Father. Father looked to me, and I ceased to look to the river. Well, let us see if we can track him. Yes, this is the corner where he got out, making a step of his trough. Thanks to the rain, his tracks are quite distinct. Here he went along the edge of the garden over the water and muskmelons, then through the beans and potatoes, and even along the front-yard walk I detect the print of his divided hoof, his two sharp toes (*ungulae*). It's a wonder we did not see him. And here he passed out under the gate, across the road, — how naked he must have felt! — into a grassy ditch, and whither next? Is it of any use to go hunting him up unless you have devised some mode of catching him when you have found? Of what avail to know where he has been, even where he is? He was so shy the little while we had him, of course he will never come back; he cannot be tempted by a swill-pail. Who knows how many miles off he is! Perhaps he has taken the back track and gone to Brighton, or Ohio! At most, probably we shall only have the satisfaction of glimpsing the nimble beast at a distance, from time to time, as he trots swiftly through the green meadows and cornfields. But, now I speak, what is that I see pacing deliberately up the middle of the street forty rods off? It is *he*. As if to tantalize, to tempt us to waste our afternoon without further hestitation, he thus offers himself. He roots a foot or two and then lies down on his belly in the middle of the street. But think not to catch him a-napping. He has his eyes about, and his ears too. He has already been chased. He gives that wagon a wide berth, and now, seeing me, he turns and trots back down the street. He turns into a front yard. Now if I can only close that gate upon him ninety-nine hundredths of the work is done, but ah! he hears me coming afar off, he foresees the danger, and, with swinish cunning and speed, he scampers out. My neighbor in the street tries to head him; he jumps to this side of the road, then to that, before him; but the third time the pig was there first and went by. "Whose is it?" he shouts. "It's ours." He bolts into that neighbor's yard and so across his premises. He has been twice there before, it seems; he knows the road; see what work he has made in his flower garden! He must be fond of bulbs. Our neighbor picks up one tall flower with its bulb attached, holds it out at arm's length. He is excited about the pig; it is a subject he is interested in. But where is [he] gone now? The last glimpse I had of him was as he went through the cow yard; here are his tracks again in this cornfield, but they are lost in the grass. We lose him; we beat the bushes in vain; he may be far away. But hark! I heard a grunt. Nevertheless for half an hour I do not see him that grunted. At last I find fresh tracks along the river, and again lose them. Each neighbor whose garden I traverse tells me some anecdote of losing pigs, or the attempt to drive them, by which I am not encouraged. Once more he crosses our first neighbor's garden and is said to be in the road. But I am not there yet; it is a good way off. At length my eyes rest on him again, after three quarters of an hour's separation. There he trots with the whole road to himself, and now again drops on his belly in a puddle. Now he starts again, seeing me twenty rods [off], deliberates, considers which way I want him to go, and goes the other. There was some chance of driving him along the sidewalk, or letting him go rather, till he slipped under our gate again, but of what avail would that be? How corner and catch him who keeps twenty rods off? He never lets the open side of the triangle be less than a dozen rods wide. There was one place where a narrower street turned off at right angles with the main one, just this side our yard, but I could not drive him past that. Twice he ran up the narrow street, for he knew I did not wish it, but though the main street was broad and open and no traveller in sight, when I tried to drive him past this opening he invariably turned his piggish head toward me, dodged from side to side, and finally ran up the narrow street, or down the main one, as if there were a high barrier erected before him. But really he is no more obstinate than I. I cannot but respect his tactics and his independence. He will be he, and I may be I. He is not unreasonable because he thwarts me, but only the more reasonable. He has a strong will. He stands upon his idea. There is a wall across the path not where a man bars the way, but where he is resolved not to travel. Is he not superior to man therein? Once more he glides down the narrow street, deliberates at a corner, chooses wisely for him, and disappears through an openwork fence eastward. He has gone to fresh gardens and pastures new. Other neighbors stand in the door-ways but half-sympathizing, only observing, "Ugly thing to catch." "You have a job on your hands." I lose sight of him, but hear that he is far ahead in a large field. And there we try to let him alone awhile, giving him a wide berth.

At this stage an Irishman was engaged to assist. "I can catch him," says he, with Buonapartean confidence. He thinks him a family Irish pig. His wife is with him, bareheaded, and his little flibbertigibbet of a boy, seven years old. "Here, Johnny, do you run right off there" (at the broadest possible angle with his own course). "Oh, but he can't do anything." "Oh, but I only want him to tell me where he is, — to keep sight of him." Michael soon discovers that he is not an Irish pig, and his wife and Johnny's occupation are soon gone. Ten minutes afterward I am patiently tracking him step by step through a cornfield, a nearsighted man helping me, and then into garden after garden far eastward, and finally into the highway, at the graveyard; but hear and see nothing. One suggests a dog to track him. Father is meanwhile selling him to the blacksmith, who also is

136

trying to get sight of him. After fifteen minutes since he disappeared eastward, I hear that he has been to the river twice far on [?] the north, through the first neighbor's premises. I wend that way. He crosses the street far ahead, Michael behind; he dodges up an avenue. I stand in the gap there, Michael at the other end, and now he tries to corner him. But it is a vain hope to corner him in a yard. I see a carriage-manufactory door open. "Let him go in there, Flannery." For once the pig and I are of one mind; he bolts in, and the door is closed. Now for a rope. It is a large barn, crowded with carriages. The rope is at length obtained; the windows are barred with carriages lest he bolt through. He is resting quietly on his belly in the further corner, thinking unutterable things.

Now the course recommences within narrower limits. Bump, bump, bump he goes, against wheels and shafts. We get no hold yet. He is all ear and eye. Small boys are sent under the carriages to drive him out. He froths at the mouth and deters them. At length he is stuck for an instant between the spokes of a wheel, and I am securely attached to his hind leg. He squeals deafeningly, and is silent. The rope is attached to a hind leg. The door is opened, and the *driving* commences. Roll an egg as well. You may drag him, but you cannot drive him. But he is in the road, and now another thunder shower greets us. I leave Michael with the rope in one hand and the switch in another and go home. He seems to be gaining a little westward. But, after long delay, I look out and find that he makes but doubtful progress.

A boy is made to face him with a stick, and it is only when the pig springs at him savagely that progress is made homeward. He will be killed before he is driven home. I get a wheelbarrow and go to the rescue. Michael is alarmed. The pig is rabid, snaps at him. We drag him across the barrow, hold him down, and so, at last, get him home.

If a wild shoat like this gets loose, first track him if you can, or otherwise discover where he is. Do not scare him more than you can help. Think of some yard or building or other enclosure that will hold him and, by showing your forces — yet as if uninterested parties — fifteen or twenty rods off, let him of his own accord enter it. Then slightly shut the gate. Now corner and tie him and put him into a cart or barrow.

All progress in driving at last was made by facing and endeavoring to switch him from home. He rushed upon you and made a few feet in the desired direction. When I approached with the barrow he advanced to meet it with determination.

So I get home at dark, wet through and supperless, covered with mud and wheel-grease, without any rare flowers.

Journal: August 8, 1856

Pig-Headed, Again

Last Friday (the 22d) afternoon (when I was away), Father's pig got out again and took to the riverside. The next day he was heard from, but not found. That night he was seen on an island in the meadow, in the midst of the flood, but thereafter for some time no account of him. J. Farmer advised to go to Ai Hale, just over the Carlisle line. He has got a dog which, if you put him on the track of the pig not more than four hours' old, will pursue and catch him and hold him by the ear without hurting him till you come up. That's the best way. Ten men cannot stop him in the road, but he will go by them. It was generally conceded that the right kind of dog was all that was wanted, like Ai Hale's, one that would hold him by the ear, but not uselessly maim him. One or two said, "If only I had such a one's dog, I'd catch him for so much."

Neighbors sympathized as much as in them lay. It was the town talk; the meetings were held at Wolcott & Holden's. Every man told of his losses and disappointments in this line. One had heard of his pig last up in Westford, but never saw him again; another had only caught his pig by his running against a post so hard as to stun himself for a few moments. It was thought this one must have been born in the woods, for he would run and leap like a wolf. Some advised not to build so very high, but lay the upper board flat over the pen, for then, when he caught by his fore feet, his body would swing under to no purpose. One said you would not catch him to buy a pig out of a drove. Our pig ran as if he *still* had the devil in him. It was generally conceded that a good dog was the desideratum. But thereupon Lawrence, the harness-maker, came forward and told his experience. He once helped hunt a pig in the next town. He weighed two hundred; had been out some time (though not in '75), but they learned where he resorted; but they got a capital dog of the right kind. They had the dog tied lest he should scare the pig too soon. They crawled along very carefully near the hollow where the pig was till they could hear him. They knew that if he should hear them and he was wide awake, he would dash off with a grunt, and that would be the last of him, but what more could they do? They consulted in a whisper and concluded to let the dog go. They did so, and directly heard an awful yelp; the pig was gone, and there lay the dog all torn to pieces! At this there was a universal *haw! haw!* and the reputation of dogs fell, and the chance of catching the pigs seemed less.

Two dollars reward was offered to him who could catch and return him without maiming him. At length, the 26th, he was heard from. He was caught and tied in north part of the town. Took to a swamp, as they say they are inclined. He was chased two hours with a spaniel dog, which never faced him, nor touched him, but, as the man said, "tuckered him out," kept him on the go and showed him where he was. When at a distance the pig stopped and faced the dog until the pursuers came up. He was brought home the 27th, all his legs tied, and put into his new pen. It was a very deep one. It might have been made deeper, but Father did not wish to build a wall, and the man who caught him and got his two dollars for it thought it ought to hold any decent pig. Father said he didn't wish to keep him in a well.

Journal: August 26, 1856.

On Cape Cod, Part 5:
Axy, Bethuel, and Shearjashub

"Now I'm going to ask you a question," said the old man, "and I don't know as you can tell me; but you are a learned man and I never had any learning, only what I got by nature." — It was in vain that we reminded him that he could quote Josephus to our confusion. — "I've thought if I ever met a learned man I should like to ask him this question. Can you tell me how *Axy* is spelt, and what it means? *Axy*," says he; "there's a girl over here is named *Axy*. Now what is it? What does it mean? Is it Scripture? I've read my Bible twenty-five years over and over, and I never came across it."

"Did you read it twenty-five years for this object?" I asked.

"Well, *how* is it spelt? Wife, how is it spelt?" She said: "It is in the Bible; I've seen it."

"Well, how do you spell it?"

"I don't know. A c h, ach, s e h, seh, — Achseh."

"Does that spell Axy? Well, do *you* know what it means?" asked he, turning to me.

"No," I replied. "I never heard the sound before."

"There was a schoolmaster down here once, and they asked him what it meant, and he said it had no more meaning than a bean-pole."

I told him that I held the same opinion with the schoolmaster. I'd been a schoolmaster myself and had had strange names to deal with. I also heard of such names as Zoheth, Beriah, Amaziah, Bethuel, and Shearjashub, hereabouts.

At length the little boy, who had a seat quite in the chimney-corner, took off his stockings and shoes, warmed his feet, and having had his sore leg freshly salved, went off to bed; then the fool made bare his knotty-looking feet and legs, and followed him; and finally the old man exposed his calves also to our gaze. We had never had the good fortune to see an old man's legs before, and were surprised to find them fair and plump as an infant's, and we thought that he took a pride in exhibiting them. He then proceeded to make preparations for retiring, discoursing meanwhile with Panurgic plainness of speech on the ills to which old humanity is subject. We were a rare haul for him. He could commonly get none but ministers to talk to, though sometimes ten of them at once, and he was glad to meet some of the laity at leisure. The evening was not long enough for him. As I had been sick, the old lady asked if I would not go to bed, — it getting late for old people; but the old man, who had not yet done his stories, said, "You ain't particular, are you?"

"Oh no," said I, "I am in no hurry. I believe I have weathered the Clam cape."

"They are good," said he; "I wish I had some of them now."

"They never hurt me," said the old lady.

"But then you took out the part that killed a cat," said I.

At last we cut him short in the midst of his stories, which he promised to resume in the morning. Yet, after all, one of the old ladies who came to our room in the night to fasten the fire-board, which rattled, as she went out took the precaution to fasten us in. Old women are by nature more suspicious than old men. ...

Cape Cod

Hats

How different are men and women, *e.g.* in respect to the adornment of their heads! Do you ever see an old or jammed bonnet on the head of a woman at a public meeting? But look at any assembly of men with their hats on; how large a proportion of the hats will be old, weatherbeaten, and indented, but I think so much the more picturesque and interesting! One farmer rides by my door in a hat which it does me good to see, there is so much character in it, — so much independence to begin with, and then affection for his old friends, etc., etc. I should not wonder if there were lichens on it. Think of painting a hero in a bran-new hat! The chief recommendation of the Kossuth hat is that it looks old to start with, and almost as good as new to end with. Indeed, it is generally conceded that a man does not look the worse for a somewhat dilapidated hat. But go to a lyceum and look at the bonnets and various other headgear of the women and girls, — who, by the way, keep their hats on, it being dangerous and expensive to take them off!! Why every one looks as fragile as a but-terfly's wings, having just come out of a bandbox, — as it will go into a bandbox again when the lyceum is over. Men wear their hats for use; women theirs for orna-ment. I have seen the greatest philosopher in the town

with what the traders would call "a shocking bad hat"
on, but the woman whose bonnet does not come up to
the mark is at best a "bluestocking."[28]

Journal: December 25, 1859

The Broad, Flapping American Ear

We are in great haste to construct a magnetic telegraph
from Maine to Texas; but Maine and Texas, it may be,
have nothing imporant to communicate. Either is in
such a predicament as the man who was earnest to be
introduced to a distinguished deaf woman, but when he
was presented, and one end of her ear trumpet was put
into his hand, had nothing to say. As if the main object
were to talk fast and not to talk sensibly. We are eager
to tunnel under the Atlantic and bring the old world
some weeks nearer to the new; but perchance the first
news that will leak through into the broad, flapping
American ear will be that the Princess Adelaide has the
whooping cough.

Walden, "Economy"

Terriers & Tints

Though the red maples have not their common brillian-
cy on account of the very severe frost about the end of
September, some are very interesting. I now see one
small red maple which is all a pure yellow within and a
bright red or scarlet on its outer surface and promi-

---

[28] An 18th-century term for an intellectual or literary woman.
Used as an insult in Thoreau's day.

nences. It is a remarkably distinct painting of scarlet on a yellow ground. It is an indescribably beautiful contrast of scarlet and yellow. Another is yellow and green where this was scarlet and yellow, and in this case the bright and liquid green, now getting to be rare, is by contrast as charming a color as the scarlet. ...

I wonder that the very cows and the dogs in the street do not manifest a recognition of the bright tints about and above them. I saw a terrier dog glance up and down the painted street before he turned in at his master's gate, and I wondered what he thought of those lit trees, — if they did not touch his philosophy or spirits, — but I fear he had only his common doggish thoughts after all. He trotted down the yard as if it were a matter of course after all, or else as if he deserved it all.[29]

Journal: October 9, 1860

Squirrel Sails

March 22, 1855. Going along the steep side-hill on the south of the pond about 4 P.M., on the edge of the little patch of wood which the choppers have not yet levelled, — though they have felled many an acre around it this winter, — I observed a rotten and hollow hemlock stump about two feet high and six inches in diameter, and instinctively approached with my right hand ready to cover it. I found a flying squirrel in it, which, as my

---

[29] It would later be widely believed that a dog's vision is black and white, but recent studies confirm that dogs do see a limited range of colors.

left hand had covered a small hole at the bottom, ran directly into my right hand. It struggled and bit not a little, but my cotton glove protected me, and I felt its teeth only once or twice. It also uttered three or four dry shrieks at first, something like *cr-r-rack cr-r-r-ack cr-r-r-ack*. I rolled it up in my handkerchief and, holding the ends tight, carried it home in my hand, some three miles. It struggled more or less all the way, especially when my feet made any unusual or louder noise going through leaves or bushes. I could count its claws as they appeared through the handkerchief, and once it got its head out a hole. It even bit through the handker-chief.

Color, as I remember, above a chestnut ash, inclin-ing to fawn or cream color (?), slightly browned; be-neath white, the under edge of its wings (?) tinged yellow, the upper dark, perhaps black, making a dark stripe. Audubon and Bachman do not speak of any such stripe! It was a very cunning little animal, reminding me of a mouse in the room. Its very large and promi-nent black eyes gave it an interesting innocent look. Its very neat flat, fawn-colored, distichous tail was a great ornament. Its "sails" were not very obvious when it was at rest, merely giving it a flat appearance beneath. It would leap off and upward into the air two or three feet from a table, spreading its "sails," and fall to the floor in vain; perhaps strike the side of the room in its upward spring and endeavor to cling to it. It would run up the windows by the sash, but evidently found the furniture and walls and floor too hard and smooth for it and after some falls became quiet. In a few moments it allowed me to stroke it, though far from confident.

I put it in a barrel and covered it for the night. It was quite busy all the evening gnawing out, clinging for this purpose and gnawing at the upper edge of a sound oak barrel, and then dropping to rest from time to time. It had defaced the barrel considerably by morning, and would probably have escaped if I had not placed a piece of iron against the gnawed part. I had left in the barrel some bread, apple, shagbarks, and cheese. It ate some of the apple and one shagbark, cutting it quite in two transversely.

In the morning it was quiet, and *squatted* somewhat curled up amid the straw, with its tail passing under it and the end curled over its head very prettily, as if to shield it from the light and keep it warm. I always found it in this position by day when I raised the lid.

March 23. P.M.—To Fair Haven Pond.

Carried my flying squirrel back to the woods in my handkerchief. I placed it, about 3.30 P.M., on the very stump I had taken it from. It immediately ran about a rod over the leaves and up under a slender maple sapling about ten feet, then after a moment's pause sprang off and skimmed downward toward a large maple nine feet distant, whose trunk it struck three or four feet from the ground. This it rapidly ascended, on the opposite side from me, nearly thirty feet, and there clung to the main stem with its head downward, eyeing me. After two or three minutes' pause I saw that it was preparing for another spring by raising its head and looking off, and away it went in admirable style, more like a bird than any quadruped I had dreamed of and far surpassing the impression I had received from naturalists' accounts. I marked the spot it started from and the place where it struck, and measured the height and distance carefully. It sprang off from the maple at the height of twenty-eight and a half feet, and struck the ground at the foot of a tree fifty and a half feet distant, measured horizontally. Its flight was not a *regular* descent; it varied from a direct line both horizontally and vertically. Indeed it skimmed much like a hawk and part of its flight was nearly horizontal, and it diverged from a right line eight or ten feet to the right, making a curve in that direction. There were six trees from six inches to a foot in diameter, one a hemlock, in a direct line between the two termini, and these it skimmed partly round, and passed through their thinner limbs; did not as I could perceive touch a twig. It skimmed its way like a hawk between and around the trees. Though it was a windy day, this was on a steep hillside away from the wind and covered with wood, so it was not aided by that. As the ground rose about two feet, the distance was to the absolute height as fifty and a half to twenty-six and a half, or it advanced about two feet for every one foot of descent. After its vain attempts in the house, I was not prepared for this exhibition. It did not fall heavily as in the house, but struck the ground gently enough, and I cannot believe that the mere extension of the skin enabled it to skim so far. It must be still fur-

ther aided by its organization. Perhaps it fills itself with
air first.

Journal: March 22-23, 1855

The Natural History
of the Cat & the Bedbug

At the Pilgrim House,[30] though it was not crowded,
they put me into a small attic chamber which had two
double beds in it, and only one window, high in a corner, twenty and a half inches by twenty-five and a half,
in the alcove when it was swung open, and it required a
chair to look out conveniently. Fortunately it was not a
cold night and the window could be kept open, though
at the risk of being visited by the cats, which appear to
swarm on the roofs of Provincetown like the mosquitoes on the summits of its hills. I have spent four memorable nights there in as many different years, and have
added considerable thereby to my knowledge of the
natural history of the cat and the bedbug. Sleep was out
of the question. A night in one of the attics of Provincetown! to say nothing of what is to be learned in entomology. It would be worth the while to send a professor
there, one who was also skilled in entomology. Such is
your *Pilgerruhe* or Pilgrims'-Rest. Every now and then
one of these animals on its travels leaped from a neighboring roof on to mine, with such a noise as if a six-
pounder had fallen within two feet of my head, — the
discharge of a catapult, — and then followed such a

---

[30] A lodging house on Cape Cod

scrambling as banished sleep for a long season, while I watched lest they came in at the open window. A kind of foretaste, methought, of the infernal regions. I did n't wonder they gave quitclaim deeds of their land there. My experience is that you fare best at private houses. The barroom may be defined a place to spit.

Journal: June 21, 1857

Sea Sweetener

March 15. Put a spout in the red maple of yesterday, and hung a pail beneath to catch the sap.

March 16. 7 A.M.—The sap of that red maple has not begun to flow yet. The few spoonfuls in the pail and in the hole are frozen.

2 P.M.—The red maple is now about an inch dep in a quart pail, — nearly all caught since morning. It now flows at the rate of about six drops in a minute. Has probably flowed faster this forenoon. It is perfectly clear, like water. Going home, slipped on the ice, throwing the pail over my head to save myself, and spilt all but a pint. So it was lost on the ice of the river. When the river breaks up, it will go down the Concord into the Merrimack, and down the Merrimack into the sea, and there get salted as well as diluted, part being boiled into sugar. It suggests, at any rate, what various liquors, beside those containing salt, find their way to the sea, — the sap of how many kinds of trees!

Journal: March 15-16, 1856

On Cape Cod, Part 6:
The Oysterman's Tobacco Juice

Before sunrise the next morning they let us out again, and I ran over to the beach to see the sun come out of the ocean. The old woman of eighty-four winters was already out in the cold morning wind, bareheaded, tripping about like a young girl, and driving up the cow to milk. She got the breakfast with despatch, and without noise or bustle; and meanwhile the old man resumed his stories, standing before us, who were sitting, with his back to the chimney, and ejecting his tobacco juice right and left into the fire behind him, without regard to the various dishes which were there preparing. At breakfast we had eels, buttermilk cake, cold bread, green beans, doughnuts, and tea. The old man talked a steady stream; and when his wife told him he had better eat his breakfast, he said: "Don't hurry me; I have lived too long to be hurried." I ate of the applesauce and the doughnuts, which I thought had sustained the lest detriment from the old man's shots, but my companion refused the applesauce, and ate of the hot cake and green beans, which had appeared to him to occupy the safest part of the hearth. But on comparing notes afterward, I told him that the buttermilk cake was particularly exposed, and I saw how it suffered repeatedly, and therefore I avoided it; but he declared that, however that might be, he witnessed that the applesauce was seriously injured, and had therefore declined that. After breakfast we looked at his clock, which was out of order, and oiled it with some "hen's grease," for want of sweet oil, for he scarcely could believe that we were not tinkers or pedlers; meanwhile he told a story about visions, which had reference to a crack in the clock-case made by frost one night. He was curious to know to what religious sect we belonged. He said that he had been to hear thirteen kinds of preaching in one month, when he was young, but he did not join any of them, — he stuck to his Bible. While I was shaving in the next room, I heard him ask my companion to what sect he belonged, to which he answered: —

"O, I belong to the Universal Brotherhood."

"What's that?" he asked, "Sons o' Temperance?"

Finally, filling our pockets with doughnuts, which he was pleased to find that we called by the same name that he did, and paying for our entertainment, we took our departure; but he followed us out of doors, and made us tell him the names of the vegetables which he had raised from seeds that came out of the *Franklin*.[31] They were cabbage, broccoli, and parsley. As I had asked him the names of so many things, he tried me in turn with all the plants which grew in his garden, both wild and cultivated. It was about half an acre, which he cultivated wholly himself. ...

As we stood there, I saw a fish-hawk stoop to pick a fish out of his pond.

"There," said I, "he has got a fish."

"Well," said the old man, who was looking all the

---

[31] The *Franklin*: a large commercial ship that wrecked on Cape Cod on March 1, 1849. The Wellfleet locals scavenged much of its spilt cargo.

while, but could see nothing, "he didn't dive, he just wet his claws."

And, sure enough, he did not this time, though it is said that they often do, but he merely stooped low enough to pick him out with his talons; but as he bore his shining prey over the bushes, it fell to the ground, and we did not see that he recovered it. That is not their practice.

Thus, having had another crack with the old man, he standing bareheaded under the eaves, he directed us "athwart the fields," and we took to the beach again for another day, it being now late in the morning.

It was but a day or two after this that the safe of the Provincetown Bank was broken open and robbed by two men from the interior, and we learned that our hospitable entertainers did at least transiently harbor the suspicion that we were the men.

… Speedy emissaries from Provincetown…traced us all the way down the Cape, and concluded that we came by [our] unusual route down the back-side and on foot, in order that we might discover a way to get off with our booty when we had committed the robbery. The Cape is so long and narrow, and so bare withal, that it is wellnigh impossible for a stranger to visit it without the knowledge of it inhabitants generally, unless he is wrecked on to it in the night. So, when this robbery occurred, all their suspicions seem to have at once centred on us two travellers who had just passed down it. If we had not chanced to leave the Cape so soon, we should probably have been arrested. The real robbers were two young men from Worcester County who travelled with a centre-bit, and are said to have done their work very neatly. But the only bank that we pried into was the great Cape Cod sand-bank, and we robbed it only of an old French crown piece, some shells and pebbles, and the materials of this story.

Cape Cod

In the Bilge-Water

Getting into Patchogue late one night in an oyster boat, there was a drunken Dutchman aboard whose wit reminded me of Shakespeare. We were detained three hours waiting for the tide, and two of the fishermen took an extra dram at the beach house. Then they stretched themselves on the seaweed by the shore in the sun to sleep off the effects. One was an inconceivably broad-faced young Dutchman, — but oh! of such a peculiar breadth and heavy look, I should not know whether to call it more ridiculous or sublime. You would say that he had humbled himself so much that he was beginning to be exalted. An indescribable mynheerish stupidity. I was less disgusted by their filthiness and vulgarity, because I was compelled to look on them as animals, as swine in their sty. For the whole voyage they lay flat on their backs on the bottom of the boat, in the bilge-water and wet with each bailing, half insensible and wallowing in their vomit. But ever and anon, when aroused by the rude kicks or curses of the skipper, the Dutchman, who never lost his wit nor equanimity, though snoring and rolling in the vomit produced by his debauch, blurted forth some happy repartee like an illuminated swine. It was the earthiest, slimiest wit I ever heard. The countenance was one of a million. It was unmistakable Dutch. In the midst of a million faces of other races it could not be mistaken. It told of Amsterdam. I kept racking my brains to conceive how he could have been born in America, how lonely he must feel, what he did for fellowship.

... There was a cross-eyed fellow used to help me survey, — he was my stake-driver, — and all he said was, at every stake he drove, "There, I shouldn't like to undertake to pull *that* up with my teeth."

It sticks in my *crop*. That's a good phrase. Many things stick there.

Journal: June 21, 1850

Bowels or Stars

I am inclined to think of late that as much depends on the state of the bowels as of the stars. As are your bowels, so are the stars.

Journal: December 12, 1859

Getting a Living [32]

At a lyceum, not long since, I felt that the lecturer had chosen a theme too foreign to himself, and so failed to interest me as much as he might have done. He described things not in or near to his heart, but toward his extremities and superficies. There was, in this sense, no truly central or centralizing thought in the lecture. I would have had him deal with his privatest experience, as the poet does. The greatest compliment that was ever paid me was when one asked me what *I thought*, and attended to my answer. I am surprised, as well as delighted, when this happens, it is such a rare use he would make of me, as if he were acquainted with the tool. Commonly, if men want anything of me, it is only to know how many acres I make of their land, — since I am a surveyor, — or, at most, what trivial news I have burdened myself with. They never will go to law for my meat; they prefer the shell. A man once came a considerable distance to ask me to lecture on Slavery; but on

---

[32] Presented as a lecture in numerous venues throughout New England beginning in Providence, Rhode Island in 1854, this text was published posthumously as an essay in *The Atlantic Monthly*, October 1863, under the title "Life without Principle." While lecturing, Thoreau presented it under various titles, including "What Shall it Profit?", "Life Misspent," "Higher Laws" (not to be confused with the chapter in *Walden* of the same title), and the title I prefer and here reinstate.

conversing with him, I found that he and his clique expected seven eighths of the lecture to be theirs, and only one eighth mine; so I declined. I take it for granted, when I am invited to lecture anywhere, — for I have had a little experience in that business, — that there is a desire to hear what *I think* on some subject, though I may be the greatest fool in the country, — and not that I should say pleasant things merely, or such as the audience will assent to; and I resolve, accordingly, that I will give them a strong dose of myself. They have sent for me, and engaged to pay for me, and I am determined that they shall have me, though I bore them beyond all precedent.

So now I would say something similar to you, my readers. Since *you* are my readers, and I have not been much of a traveller, I will not talk about people a thousand miles off, but come as near home as I can. As the time is short, I will leave out all the flattery, and retain all the criticism.

Let us consider the way in which we spend our lives.

This world is a place of business. What an infinite bustle! I am awaked almost every night by the panting of the locomotive. It interrupts my dreams. There is no sabbath. It would be glorious to see mankind at leisure for once. It is nothing but work, work, work. I cannot easily buy a blank-book to write thoughts in; they are commonly ruled for dollars and cents. An Irishman, seeing me making a minute in the fields, took it for granted that I was calculating my wages. If a man was tossed out of a window when an infant, and so made a cripple for life, or seared out of his wits by the Indians, it is regretted chiefly because he was thus incapacitated for — business! I think that there is nothing, not even crime, more opposed to poetry, to philosophy, ay, to life itself, than this incessant business.

There is a coarse and boisterous money-making fellow in the outskirts of our town, who is going to build a bank-wall under the hill along the edge of his meadow. The powers have put this into his head to keep him out of mischief, and he wishes me to spend three weeks digging there with him. The result will be that he will perhaps get some more money to board, and leave for his heirs to spend foolishly. If I do this, most will commend me as an industrious and hard-working man; but if I choose to devote myself to certain labors which yield more real profit, though but little money, they may be inclined to look on me as an idler. Nevertheless, as I do not need the police of meaningless labor to regulate me, and do not see anything absolutely praiseworthy in this fellow's undertaking any more than in many an enterprise of our own or foreign governments, however amusing it may be to him or them, I prefer to finish my education at a different school.

If a man walk in the woods for love of them half of each day, he is in danger of being regarded as a loafer; but if he spends his whole day as a speculator, shearing off those woods and making earth bald before her time, he is esteemed an industrious and enterprising citizen.

As if a town had no interest in its forests but to cut them down!

Most men would feel insulted, if it were proposed to employ them in throwing stones over a wall, and then in throwing them back, merely that they might earn their wages. But many are no more worthily employed now. For instance: just after sunrise, one summer morning, I noticed one of my neighbors walking beside his team, which was slowly drawing a heavy hewn stone swung under the axle, surrounded by an atmosphere of industry, — his day's work begun, — his brow commenced to sweat, — a reproach to all sluggards and idlers, — pausing abreast the shoulders of his oxen, and half turning round with a flourish of his merciful whip, while they gained their length on him. And I thought, Such is the labor which the American Congress exists to protect, — honest, manly toil, — honest as the day is long, — that makes his bread taste sweet, and keeps society sweet, — which all men respect and have consecrated: one of the sacred band, doing the needful but irksome drudgery. Indeed, I felt a slight reproach, because I observed this from a window, and was not abroad and stirring about a similar business. The day went by, and at evening I passed the yard of another neighbor, who keeps many servants, and spends much money foolishly, while he adds nothing to the common stock, and there I saw the stone of the morning lying beside a whimsical structure intended to adorn this Lord Timothy Dexter's[33] premises, and the dignity forthwith departed from the teamster's labor, in my eyes. In my opinion, the sun was made to light worthier toil than this. I may add that his employer has since run off, in debt to a good part of the town, and, after passing through Chancery, has settled somewhere else, there to become once more a patron of the arts.

The ways by which you may get money almost without exception lead downward. To have done anything by which you earned money *merely* is to have been truly idle or worse. If the laborer gets no more than the wages which his employer pays him, he is cheated, he cheats himself. If you would get money as a writer or lecturer, you must be popular, which is to go down perpendicularly. Those services which the community will most readily pay for, it is most disagreeable to render. You are paid for being something less than a man. The State does not commonly reward a genius any more wisely. Even the poet-laureate would rather not have to celebrate the accidents of royalty. He must be bribed with a pipe of wine; and perhaps another poet is called away from his muse to gauge that very pipe. As for my own business, even that kind of surveying which I could do with most satisfaction my employers do not want. They would prefer that I should do my work coarsely and not too well, ay, not well enough. When I

---

[33] Lord Timothy Dexter (1747-1806): A notably eccentric Massachussets business man who decorated his Newburyport house with minarets, an eagle-topped cupola, and an outlandish array of statues in the garden.

observe that there are different ways of surveying, my employer commonly asks which will give him the most land, not which is most correct. I once invented a rule for measuring cord-wood, and tried to introduce it in Boston; but the measurer there told me that the sellers did not wish to have their wood measured correctly, — that he was already too accurate for them, and therefore they commonly got their wood measured in Charlestown before crossing the bridge.

The aim of the laborer should be, not to get his living, to get "a good job," but to perform well a certain work; and, even in a pecuniary sense, it would be economy for a town to pay its laborers so well that they would not feel that they were working for low ends, as for a livelihood merely, but for scientific, or even moral ends. Do not hire a man who does your work for money, but him who does it for love of it.

It is remarkable that there are few men so well employed, so much to their minds, but that a little money or fame would commonly buy them off from their present pursuit. I see advertisements for *active* young men, as if activity were the whole of a young man's capital. Yet I have been surprised when one has with confidence proposed to me, a grown man, to embark in some enterprise of his, as if I had absolutely nothing to do, my life having been a complete failure hitherto. What a doubtful compliment this is to pay me! As if he had met me half-way across the ocean beating up against the wind, but bound nowhere, and proposed to me to go along with him! If I did, what do you think the underwriters would say? No, no! I am not without employment at this stage of the voyage. To tell the truth, I saw an advertisement for able-bodied seamen, when I was a boy, sauntering in my native port, and as soon as I came of age I embarked.

The community has no bribe that will tempt a wise man. You may raise money enough to tunnel a mountain, but you cannot raise money enough to hire a man who is minding his *own* business. An efficient and valuable man does what he can, whether the community pay him for it or not. The inefficient offer their inefficiency to the highest bidder, and are forever expecting to be put into office. One would suppose that they were rarely disappointed.

Perhaps I am more than usually jealous with respect to my freedom. I feel that my connection with and obligation to society are still very slight and transient. Those slight labors which afford me a livelihood, and by which it is allowed that I am to some extent serviceable to my contemporaries, are as yet commonly a pleasure to me, and I am not often reminded that they are a necessity. So far I am successful. But I foresee, that, if my wants should be much increased, the labor required to supply them would become a drudgery. If I should sell both my forenoons and afternoons to society, as most appear to do, I am sure that for me there would be nothing left worth living for. I trust that I shall never thus sell my birthright for a mess of pottage. I wish to suggest that a man may be very industrious, and yet not spend his time well. There is no more fatal blunderer than he who consumes the greater part of his life getting his living. All great enterprises are self-supporting. The poet, for instance, must sustain his body by his poetry, as a steam planing-mill feeds its boilers with the shavings it makes. You must get your living by loving. But as it is said of the merchants that ninety-seven in a hundred fail, so the life of men generally, tried by this standard, is a failure, and bankruptcy may be surely prophesied.

Merely to come into the world the heir of a fortune is not to be born, but to be still-born, rather. To be supported by the charity of friends, or a government pension, — provided you continue to breathe, — by whatever fine synonymes you describe these relations, is to go into the almshouse. On Sundays the poor debtor goes to church to take an account of stock, and finds, of course, that his outgoes have been greater than his income. In the Catholic Church, especially, they go into chancery, make a clean confession, give up all, and think to start again. Thus men will lie on their backs, talking about the fall of man, and never make an effort to get up.

As for the comparative demand which men make on life, it is an important difference between two, that the one is satisfied with a level success, that his marks can all be hit by point-blank shots, but the other, however low and unsuccessful his life may be, constantly elevates his aim, though at a very slight angle to the horizon. I should much rather be the last man, — though, as the Orientals say, "Greatness doth not approach him who is forever looking down; and all those who are looking high are growing poor."

It is remarkable that there is little or nothing to be remembered written on the subject of getting a living: how to make getting a living not merely honest and honorable, but altogether inviting and glorious; for if *getting* a living is not so, then living is not. One would think, from looking at literature, that this question had never disturbed a solitary individual's musings. Is it that men are too much disgusted with their experience to speak of it? The lesson of value which money teaches, which the Author of the Universe has taken so much pains to teach us, we are inclined to skip altogether. As for the means of living, it is wonderful how indifferent men of all classes are about it, even reformers, so called, — whether they inherit, or earn, or steal it. I think that society has done nothing for us in this respect, or at least has undone what she has done. Cold and hunger seem more friendly to my nature than those methods which men have adopted and advise to ward them off.

The title *wise* is, for the most part, falsely applied. How can one be a wise man, if he does not know any better how to live than other men? — if he is only more cunning and intellectually subtle? Does Wisdom work in a tread-mill? or does she teach how to succeed by *her example*? Is there any such thing as wisdom not applied to life? Is she merely the miller who grinds the finest logic? It is pertinent to ask if Plato got his *living* in a better way or more successfully than his contemporaries, — or did he succumb to the difficulties of life like other men? Did he seem to prevail over some of them merely by indifference, or by assuming grand airs? or find it easier to live, because his aunt remembered him in her will? The ways in which most men get their living, that is, live, are mere makeshifts, and a shirking of the real business of life, — chiefly because they do not know, but partly because they do not mean, any better.

The rush to California, for instance, and the attitude, not merely of merchants, but of philosophers and prophets, so called, in relation to it, reflect the greatest disgrace on mankind. That so many are ready to live by luck, and so get the means of commanding the labor of others less lucky, without contributing any value to society! And that is called enterprise! I know of no more startling development of the immorality of trade, and all the common modes of getting a living. The philosophy and poetry and religion of such a mankind are not worth the dust of a puffball. The hog that gets his living by rooting, stirring up the soil so, would be ashamed of such company. If I could command the wealth of all the worlds by lifting my finger, I would not pay *such* a price for it. Even Mahomet knew that God did not make this world in jest. It makes God to be a moneyed gentleman who scatters a handful of pennies in order to see mankind scramble for them. The world's raffle! A subsistence in the domains of Nature a thing to be raffled for! What a comment, what a satire, on our institutions! The conclusion will be, that mankind will hang itself upon a tree. And have all the precepts in all the Bibles taught men only this? and is the last and most admirable invention of the human race only an improved muck-rake? Is this the ground on which Orientals and Occidentals meet? Did God direct us so to get our living, digging where we never planted, — and He would, perchance, reward us with lumps of gold?

God gave the righteous man a certificate entitling him to food and raiment, but the unrighteous man found a *facsimile* of the same in God's coffers, and appropriated it, and obtained food and raiment like the former. It is one of the most extensive systems of counterfeiting that the world has seen. I did not know that mankind was suffering for want of gold. I have seen a little of it. I know that it is very malleable, but not so malleable as wit. A grain of gold will gild a great surface, but not so much as a grain of wisdom.

The gold-digger in the ravines of the mountains is as much a gambler as his fellow in the saloons of San Francisco. What difference does it make, whether you shake dirt or shake dice? If you win, society is the loser. The gold-digger is the enemy of the honest laborer, whatever checks and compensations there may be. It is not enough to tell me that you worked hard to get your gold. So does the Devil work hard. The way of transgressors may be hard in many respects. The humblest observer who goes to the mines sees and says that gold-digging is of the character of a lottery; the gold thus obtained is not the same same thing with the wages of honest toil. But, practically, he forgets what he has seen, for he has seen only the fact, not the principle, and goes into trade there, that is, buys a ticket in what commonly proves another lottery, where the fact is not so obvious.

After reading Howitt's account of the Australian gold-diggings one evening, I had in my mind's eye, all night, the numerous valleys, with their streams, all cut up with foul pits, from ten to one hundred feet deep, and half a dozen feet across, as close as they can be dug, and partly filled with water, — the locality to which men furiously rush to probe for their fortunes, — uncertain where they shall break ground, — not knowing but the gold is under their camp itself, — sometimes digging one hundred and sixty feet before they strike the vein, or then missing it by a foot, — turned into demons, and regardless of each others' rights, in their thirst for riches, — whole valleys, for thirty miles, suddenly honeycombed by the pits of the miners, so that even hundreds are drowned in them, — standing in water, and covered with mud and clay, they work night and day, dying of exposure and disease. Having read this, and partly forgotten it, I was think-ing, accidentally, of my own unsatisfactory life, doing as others do; and with that vision of the diggings still before me, I asked myself why I might not be washing some gold daily, though it were only the finest part-icles, — why *I* might not sink a shaft down to the gold within me, and work that mine. *There* is a Ballarat, a

Bendigo[34] for you, — what though it were a sulky-gully? At any rate, I might pursue some path, however solitary and narrow and crooked, in which I could walk with love and reverence. Wherever a man separates from the multitude, and goes his own way in this mood, there indeed is a fork in the road, though ordinary travellers may see only a gap in the paling. His solitary path across-lots will turn out the *higher way* of the two.

Men rush to California and Australia as if the true gold were to be found in that direction; but that is to go to the very opposite extreme to where it lies. They go prospecting farther and farther away from the true lead, and are most unfortunate when they think themselves most successful. Is not our *native* soil auriferous? Does not a stream from the golden mountains flow through our native valley? and has not this for more than geologic ages been bringing down the shining particles and forming the nuggets for us? Yet, strange to tell, if a digger steal away, prospecting for this true gold, into the unexplored solitudes around us, there is no danger that any will dog his steps, and endeavor to supplant him. He may claim and undermine the whole valley even, both the cultivated and the uncultivated portions, his whole life long in peace, for no one will ever dispute his claim. They will not mind his cradles or his toms.[35] He is not confined to a claim twelve feet square, as at

---

[34] Ballarat, Bendigo: cities in Victoria, Australia, boasting some of the richest gold deposits on earth
[35] Cradles, Toms: mechanisms for sifting gold while mining

Ballarat, but may mine anywhere, and wash the whole wide world in his tom.

Howitt says of the man who found the great nugget which weighed twenty-eight pounds, at the Bendigo diggings in Australia: "He soon began to drink; got a horse, and rode all about, generally at full gallop, and, when he met people, called out to inquire if they knew who he was, and then kindly informed them that he was 'the bloody wretch that had found the nugget.' At last he rode full speed against a tree, and nearly knocked his brains out." I think, however, there was no danger of that, for he had already knocked his brains out against the nugget. Howitt adds, "He is a hopelessly ruined man." But he is a type of the class. They are all fast men. Hear some of the names of the places where they dig: "Jackass Flat," — "Sheep's-Head Gully," — "Murderer's Bar," etc. Is there no satire in these names?[36] Let them carry their ill-gotten wealth where they will, I am thinking it will still be "Jackass Flat," if not "Murderer's Bar," where they live.

The last resource of our energy has been the robbing of graveyards on the Isthmus of Darien,[37] an enterprise which appears to be but in its infancy; for, according to late accounts, an act has passed its second reading in the legislature of New Granada, regulating this kind of mining; and a correspondent of the "Trib-

---

[36] Consider also: "Silicon Valley"
[37] Isthmus of Darien: Panama today. Presumably Thoreau is referring to the raiding of gold from indigenous graves by prospectors in the region.

une" writes: — "In the dry season, when the weather will permit of the country being properly prospected, no doubt other rich '*guacas*' [that is, graveyards] will be found." To emigrants he says: — "Do not come before December; take the Isthmus route in preference to the Boca del Toro one; bring no useless baggage, and do not cumber yourself with a tent; but a good pair of blankets will be necessary; a pick, shovel, and axe of good material will be almost all that is required": advice which might have been taken from the "Burker's Guide." And he concludes with this line in Italics and small capitals: "*If you are doing well at home,* STAY THERE," which may fairly be interpreted to mean, "If you are getting a good living by robbing graveyards at home, stay there."

But why go to California for a text? She is the child of New England, bred at her own school and church.

It is remarkable that among all the preachers there are so few moral teachers. The prophets are employed in excusing the ways of men. Most reverend seniors, the *illuminati* of the age, tell me, with a gracious, reminiscent smile, betwixt an aspiration and a shudder, not to be too tender about these things, — to lump all that, that is, make a lump of gold of it. The highest advice I have heard on these subjects was grovelling. The burden of it was, — It is not worth your while to undertake to reform the world in this particular. Do not ask how your bread is buttered; it will make you sick, if you do, — and the like. A man had better starve at once than lose his innocence in the process of getting his bread. If

within the sophisticated man there is not an unsophist-
icated one, then he is but one of the Devil's angels. As
we grow old, we live more coarsely, we relax a little in
our disciplines, and, to some extent, cease to obey our
finest instincts. But we should be fastidious to the
extreme of sanity, disregarding the gibes of those who
are more unfortunate than ourselves.

In our science and philosophy, even, there is commonly no true and absolute account of things. The
spirit of sect and bigotry has planted its hoof amid the
stars. You have only to discuss the problem, whether
the stars are inhabited or not, in order to discover it.
Why must we daub the heavens as well as the earth? It
was an unfortunate discovery that Dr. Kane was a
Mason, and that Sir John Franklin[38] was another. But it
was a more cruel suggestion that possibly that was the
reason why the former went in search of the latter.
There is not a popular magazine in this country that
would dare to print a child's thought on important
subjects without comment. It must be submitted to the
D.D.s.[39] I would it were the chickadee-dees.

You come from attending the funeral of mankind to
attend to a natural phenomenon. A little thought is
sexton to all the world.

---

[38] Sir John Franklin (1786-1847), an officer of the British Royal
Navy, disappeared (and died) in the Canadian Arctic during an
1847 expedition. Dr. Elisha Kent Kane (1820-1857), a U.S. Navy
surgeon and explorer, was involved in two unsuccessful
expeditions to find Franklin.
[39] D.D.: Doctor of Divinity, an honorary degree

I hardly know an *intellectual* man, even, who is so broad and truly liberal that you can think aloud in his society. Most with whom you endeavor to talk soon come to a stand against some institution in which they appear to hold stock, — that is, some particular, not universal, way of viewing things. They will continually thrust their own low roof, with its narrow skylight, between you and the sky, when it is the unobstructed heavens you would view. Get out of the way with your cobwebs, wash your windows, I say! In some lyceums they tell me that they have voted to exclude the subject of religion. But how do I know what their religion is, and when I am near to or far from it? I have walked into such an arena and done my best to make a clean breast of what religion I have experienced, and the audience never suspected what I was about. The lecture was as harmless as moonshine to them. Whereas, if I had read to them the biography of the greatest scamps in history, they might have thought that I had written the lives of the deacons of their church. Ordinarily, the inquiry is, Where did you come from? or, Where are you going? That was a more pertinent question which I overheard one of my auditors put to another once, — "What does he lecture for?" It made me quake in my shoes.

To speak impartially, the best men that I know are not serene, a world in themselves. For the most part, they dwell in forms, and flatter and study effect only more finely than the rest. We select granite for the underpinning of our houses and barns; we build fences

of stone; but we do not ourselves rest on an underpinning of granitic truth, the lowest primitive rock. Our
sills are rotten. What stuff is the man made of who is
not coexistent in our thought with the purest and
subtilest truth? I often accuse my finest acquaintances
of an immense frivolity; for, while there are manners
and compliments we do not meet, we do not teach one
another the lessons of honesty and sincerity that the
brutes do, or of steadiness and solidity that the rocks
do. The fault is commonly mutual, however; for we do
not habitually demand any more of each other.

That excitement about Kossuth,[40] consider how
characteristic, but superficial, it was! — only another
kind of politics or dancing. Men were making speeches
to him all over the country, but each expressed only the
thought, or the want of thought, of the multitude. No
man stood on truth. They were merely banded together, as usual, one leaning on another, and all together on

---

[40] Lajos Kossuth (1802-1894), known as the Father of
Hungarian Democracy. A Hungarian lawyer, journalist, and
orator, he was briefly Regent-President of Hungary during that
country's revolution of 1849 against the Hapsburgs. Kossuth
was renowned for his public speeches and hailed in his own time
in Europe and abroad as a defender of liberty. In 1851-52,
during a visit eagerly anticipated by American abolitionists who
hoped his message of freedom would reverberate in support of
the cause of America's slaves, he toured several U.S. states and
met with President Fillmore. Arriving in New York City, he
received as a gift from hatter and shrewd businessman John
Genin a broad-brimmed slouch hat adorned with an ostrich
feather, dubbed the "Kossuth Hat" in his honor. The hat
received much attention in the press and brought Genin
immense profits.

nothing; as the Hindoos made the world rest on an elephant, the elephant on a tortoise, and the tortoise on a
serpent, and had nothing to put under the serpent. For
all fruit of that stir we have the Kossuth hat.

Just so hollow and ineffectual, for the most part, is
our ordinary conversation. Surface meets surface. When
our life ceases to be inward and private, conversation
degenerates into mere gossip. We rarely meet a man
who can tell us any news which he has not read in a
newspaper, or been told by his neighbor; and, for the
most part, the only difference between us and our fellow
is, that he has seen the newspaper, or been out to tea,
and we have not. In proportion as our inward life fails,
we go more constantly and desperately to the post-
office.[41] You may depend on it, that the poor fellow who
walks away with the greatest number of letters, proud
of his extensive correspondence, has not heard from
himself this long while.

I do not know but it is too much to read one newspaper a week. I have tried it recently, and for so long it
seems to me that I have not dwelt in my native region.
The sun, the clouds, the snow, the trees say not so
much to me. You cannot serve two masters. It requires
more than a day's devotion to know and to possess the
wealth of a day.

We may well be ashamed to tell what things we
have read or heard in our day. I did not know why my
news should be so trivial, — considering what one's

---

[41] E-mail or Facebook today.

dreams and expectations are, why the developments should be so paltry. The news we hear, for the most part, is not news to our genius. It is the stalest repetition. You are often tempted to ask, why such stress is laid on a particular experience which you have had, — that, after twenty-five years, you should meet Hobbins, Registrar of Deeds, again on the sidewalk. Have you not budged an inch, then? Such is the daily news. Its facts appear to float in the atmosphere, insignificant as the sporules of fungi, and impinge on some neglected *thallus*, or surface of our minds, which affords a basis for them, and hence a parasitic growth. We should wash ourselves clean of such news. Of what consequence, though our planet explode, if there is no character involved in the explosion? In health we have not the least curiosity about such events. We do not live for idle amusement. I would not run round a corner to see the world blow up.

All summer, and far into the autumn, perchance, you unconsciously went by the newspapers and the news, and now you find it was because the morning and the evening were full of news to you. Your walks were full of incidents. You attended, not to the affairs of Europe, but to your own affairs in Massachusetts fields. If you chance to live and move and have your being in that thin stratum in which the events that make the news transpire, — thinner than the paper on which it is printed, — then these things will fill the world for you; but if you soar above or dive below that plane, you cannot remember nor be reminded of them. Really to see the sun rise or go down every day, so to relate ourselves to a universal fact, would preserve us sane forever. Nations! What are nations? Tartars, and Huns, and Chinamen! Like insects, they swarm. The historian strives in vain to make them memorable. It is for want of a man that there are so many men. It is individuals that populate the world. Any man thinking may say with the Spirit of Lodin, —

> "I look down from my height on nations,
>   And they become ashes before me; —
>   Calm is my dwelling in the clouds;
> Pleasant are the great fields of my rest."[42]

Pray, let us live without being drawn by dogs, Esquimaux-fashion, tearing over hill and dale, and biting each other's ears.

Not without a slight shudder at the danger, I often perceive how near I had come to admitting into my mind the details of some trivial affair, — the news of the street; and I am astonished to observe how willing men are to lumber their minds with such rubbish, — to permit idle rumors and incidents of the most insignificant kind to intrude on ground which should be sacred to thought. Shall the mind be a public arena, where the affairs of the street and the gossip of the tea-table chiefly are discussed? Or shall it be a quarter of heaven

---

[42] From the poems of Ossian, an epic cycle by 18th-century Scottish poet James MacPherson based in Gaelic mythology.

itself, — an hypaethral temple, consecrated to the service of the gods? I find it so difficult to dispose of the few facts which to me are significant, that I hesitate to burden my attention with those which are insignificant, which only a divine mind could illustrate. Such is, for the most part, the news in newspapers and conversation. It is important to preserve the mind's chastity in this respect. Think of admitting the details of a single case of the criminal court into our thoughts, to stalk profanely through their very *sanctum sanctorum* for an hour, ay, for many hours! to make a very bar-room of the mind's inmost apartment, as if for so long the dust of the street had occupied us, — the very street itself, with all its travel, its bustle, and filth, had passed through our thoughts' shrine! Would it not be an intellectual and moral suicide? When I have been compelled to sit spectator and auditor in a court-room for some hours, and have seen my neighbors, who were not compelled, stealing in from time to time, and tiptoeing about with washed hands and faces, it has appeared to my mind's eye, that, when they took off their hats, their ears suddenly expanded into vast hoppers for sound, between which even their narrow heads were crowded. Like the vanes of windmills, they caught the broad but shallow stream of sound, which, after a few titillating gyrations in their coggy brains, passed out the other side. I wondered if, when they got home, they were as careful to wash their ears as before their hands and faces. It has seemed to me, at such a time, that the auditors and the witnesses, the jury and the counsel, the judge and the criminal at the bar, — if I may presume him guilty before he is convicted, — were all equally criminal, and a thunderbolt might be expected to descend and consume them all together.

By all kinds of traps and sign-boards, threatening the extreme penalty of the divine law, exclude such trespassers from the only ground which can be sacred to you. It is so hard to forget what it is worse than useless to remember! If I am to be a thoroughfare, I prefer that it be of the mountain brooks, the Parnassian streams, and not the town-sewers. There is inspiration, that gossip which comes to the ear of the attentive mind from the courts of heaven. There is the profane and stale revelation of the bar-room and the police court. The same ear is fitted to receive both communications. Only the character of the hearer determines to which it shall be open, and to which closed. I believe that the mind can be permanently profaned by the habit of attending to trivial things, so that all our thoughts shall be tinged with triviality. Our very intellect shall be macadamized, as it were, — its foundation broken into fragments for the wheels of travel to roll over; and if you would know what will make the most durable pavement, surpassing rolled stones, spruce blocks, and asphaltum, you have only to look into some of our minds which have been subjected to this treatment so long.

If we have thus desecrated ourselves, — as who has not? — the remedy will be by wariness and devotion to reconsecrate ourselves, and make once more a fane[43] of the mind. We should treat our minds, that is, ourselves, as innocent and ingenuous children, whose guardians we are, and be careful what objects and what subjects we thrust on their attention. Read not the Times. Read the Eternities. Conventionalities are at length as bad as impurities. Even the facts of science may dust the mind by their dryness, unless they are in a sense effaced each morning, or rather rendered fertile by the dews of fresh and living truth. Knowledge does not come to us by details, but in flashes of light from heaven. Yes, every thought that passes through the mind helps to wear and tear it, and to deepen the ruts, which, as in the streets of Pompeii, evince how much it has been used.[44] How many things there are concerning which we might well deliberate, whether we had better know them, — had better let their peddling-carts be driven, even at the slowest trot or walk, over that bridge of glorious span by which we trust to pass at last from the farthest brink of time to the nearest shore of eternity! Have we no culture, no refinement, — but skill only to live coarsely and serve the Devil? — to acquire a little worldly wealth, or fame, or liberty, and make a false show with it, as if we were all husk and shell, with no tender and living kernel to us? Shall our institutions be like those

---

[43] A temple

[44] In many ways, Thoreau's moral/aesthetic concerns about the "desecration" of the mind by trivia anticipate the insights about brain function recently afforded us through the scientific discovery of neuroplasticity.

chestnut-burs which contain abortive nuts, perfect only to prick the fingers?

America is said to be the arena on which the battle of freedom is to be fought; but surely it cannot be freedom in a merely political sense that is meant. Even if we grant that the American has freed himself from a political tyrant, he is still the slave of an economical and moral tyrant. Now that the republic — the *res-publica* — has been settled, it is time to look after the *res-privata*, — the private state, — to see, as the Roman senate charged its consuls, "*ne quid res*-PRIVATA *detrimenti caperet*," that the *private* state receive no detriment.

Do we call this the land of the free? What is it to be free from King George and continue the slaves of King Prejudice? What is it to be born free and not to live free? What is the value of any political freedom, but as a means to moral freedom? Is it a freedom to be slaves, or a freedom to be free, of which we boast? We are a nation of politicians, concerned about the outmost defences only of freedom. It is our children's children who may perchance be really free. We tax ourselves unjustly. There is a part of us which is not represented. It is taxation without representation. We quarter troops, we quarter fools and cattle of all sorts upon ourselves. We quarter our gross bodies on our poor souls, till the former eat up all the latter's substance.

With respect to a true culture and manhood, we are essentially provincial still, not metropolitan, — mere Jonathans. We are provincial, because we do not find at home our standards, — because we do not worship truth, but the reflection of truth, — because we are warped and narrowed by an exclusive devotion to trade and commerce and manufactures and agriculture and the like, which are but means, and not the end.

So is the English Parliament provincial. Mere country-bumpkins, they betray themselves, when any more important question arises for them to settle, the Irish question, for instance, — the English question why did I not say? Their natures are subdued to what they work in. Their "good breeding" respects only secondary objects. The finest manners in the world are awkwardness and fatuity when contrasted with a finer intelligence. They appear but as the fashions of past days, — mere courtliness, knee-buckles and small-clothes, out of date. It is the vice, but not the excellence of manners, that they are continually being deserted by the character; they are cast-off clothes or shells, claiming the respect which belonged to the living creature. You are presented with the shells instead of the meat, and it is no excuse generally, that, in the case of some fishes, the shells are of more worth than the meat. The man who thrusts his manners upon me does as if he were to insist on introducing me to his cabinet of curiosities, when I wished to see himself. It was not in this sense that the poet Decker called Christ "the first true gentleman that ever breathed." I repeat that in this sense the most splendid court in Christendom is provincial, having authority to consult about Trans-alpine interests only, and not the affairs of Rome. A praetor or proconsul would suffice to settle the questions which absorb the attention of the English Parliament and the American Congress.

Government and legislation! these I thought were respectable professions. We have heard of heaven-born Numas, Lycurguses, and Solons,[45] in the history of the world, whose *names* at least may stand for ideal legislators; but think of legislating to *regulate* the breeding of slaves, or the exportation of tobacco! What have divine legislators to do with the exportation or the importation of tobacco? what humane ones with the breeding of slaves? Suppose you were to submit the question to any son of God, — and has He no children in the nineteenth century? is it a family which is extinct? — in what condition would you get it again? What shall a State like Virginia say for itself at the last day, in which these have been the principal, the staple productions? What ground is there for patriotism in such a State? I derive my facts from statistical tables which the States themselves have published.

A commerce that whitens every sea in quest of nuts and raisins, and makes slaves of its sailors for this purpose! I saw, the other day, a vessel which had been wrecked, and many lives lost, and her cargo of rags, juniper-berries, and bitter almonds were strewn along the shore. It seemed hardly worth the while to tempt the dangers of the sea between Leghorn and New York for the sake of a cargo of juniper-berries and bitter

---

[45] Numa Pompilius, Lycurgus, Solon: wise law-makers of Rome, Sparta, and Athens respectively

almonds. America sending to the Old World for her bitters! Is not the sea-brine, is not shipwreck, bitter enough to make the cup of life go down here? Yet such, to a great extent, is our boasted commerce; and there are those who style themselves statesmen and philosophers who are so blind as to think that progress and civilization depend on precisely this kind of interchange and activity, — the activity of flies about a molasses-hogshead. Very well, observes one, if men were oysters. And very well, answer I, if men were mosquitoes.

Lieutenant Herndon, whom our government sent to explore the Amazon, and, it is said, to extend the area of Slavery, observed that there was wanting there "an industrious and active population, who know what the comforts of life are, and who have artificial wants to draw out the great resources of the country." But what are the "artificial wants" to be encouraged? Not the love of luxuries, like the tobacco and slaves of, I believe, his native Virginia, nor the ice and granite and other material wealth of our native New England; nor are "the great resources of a country" that fertility or barrenness of soil which produces these. The chief want, in every State that I have been into, was a high and earnest purpose in its inhabitants. This alone draws out "the great resources" of Nature, and at last taxes her beyond her resources; for man naturally dies out of her. When we want culture more than potatoes, and illumination more than sugar-plums, then the great resources of a world are taxed and drawn out, and the result, or staple production, is, not slaves, nor operatives, but men, —

those rare fruits called heroes, saints, poets, philoso-phers, and redeemers.

In short, as a snow-drift is formed where there is a lull in the wind, so, one would say, where there is a lull of truth, an institution springs up. But the truth blows right on over it, nevertheless, and at length blows it down.

What is called politics is comparatively something so superficial and inhuman, that, practically, I have never fairly recognized that it concerns me at all. The newspapers, I perceive, devote some of their columns specially to politics or government without charge; and this, one would say, is all that saves it; but, as I love literature, and, to some extent, the truth also, I never read those columns at any rate. I do not wish to blunt my sense of right so much. I have not got to answer for having read a single President's Message. A strange age of the world this, when empires, kingdoms, and republics come a-begging to a private man's door, and utter their complaints at his elbow! I cannot take up a newspaper but I find that some wretched government or other, hard pushed, and on its last legs, is interced-ing with me, the reader, to vote for it, — more importu-nate than an Italian beggar; and if I have a mind to look at its certificate, made, perchance, by some benevolent merchant's clerk, or the skipper that brought it over, for it cannot speak a word of English itself, I shall probably read of the eruption of some Vesuvius, or the overflowing of some Po, true or forged, which brought it into this condition. I do not hesitate, in such a case, to suggest work, or the almshouse; or why not keep its castle in silence, as I do commonly? The poor President, what with preserving his popularity and doing his duty, is completely bewildered. The newspapers are the ruling power. Any other government is reduced to a few marines at Fort Independence. If a man neglects to read the Daily Times, government will go down on its knees to him, for this is the only treason in these days.

Those things which now most engage the attention of men, as politics and the daily routine, are, it is true, vital functions of human society, but should be unconsciously performed, like the corresponding functions of the physical body. They are *infra*-human, a kind of vegetation. I sometimes awake to a half-consciousness of them going on about me, as a man may become conscious of some of the processes of digestion in a morbid state, and so have the dyspepsia, as it is called. It is as if a thinker submitted himself to be rasped by the great gizzard of creation. Politics is, as it were, the gizzard of society, full of grit and gravel, and the two political parties are its two opposite halves, — sometimes split into quarters, it may be, which grind on each other. Not only individuals, but states, have thus a confirmed dyspepsia, which expresses itself, you can imagine by what sort of eloquence. Thus our life is not altogether a forgetting, but also, alas! to a great extent, a remembering of that which we should never have been conscious of, certainly not in our waking hours. Why should we not meet, not always as dyspeptics, to tell our bad dreams, but sometimes as *eu*peptics, to congratulate each other on the ever glorious morning? I do not make an exorbitant demand, surely.

SELECTED BIBLIOGRAPHY

The Annotated Walden, ed. Philip Van Doren Stern
(Barnes & Noble Books, 1992)
Cape Cod (Apollo Editions, 1966)
Civil Disobedience and Other Essays
(Dover Publications, 1993)
The Days of Henry Thoreau by Walter Harding (Dover
Publications, 1982)
H.D. Thoreau: A Writer's Journal, ed. Laurence Stapleton
(Dover Publications, 1960)
The Heart of Thoreau's Journals, ed. Odell Shepard
(Dover Publications, 1961)
*I to Myself: An Annotated Selection from the Journal of
Henry D. Thoreau*, ed. Jeffrey S. Cramer (Yale
University Press, 2007)
The Journal: 1837-1861, ed. Damion Searls (New York
Review Books, 2009)
Selections from the Journals, ed. Walter Harding (Dover
Publications, 1995)
Walden and Civil Disobedience (Penguin Books, 1983)

FURTHER RECOMMENDED READING:
Emerson Among the Eccentrics by Carlos Baker
Henry Thoreau: A Life of the Mind by Robert D.
Richardson
The Maine Woods by Henry David Thoreau
The Portable Emerson, ed. Carl Bode
The Transcendentalists, ed. Perry Miller